E/572

JAMIE'S

Jamie's Way

Stories for Worship and Family Devotion

SUSAN C. HARRISS

COWLEY PUBLICATIONS
Cambridge, Massachusetts

FORWARD MOVEMENT PUBLICATIONS
Cincinnati, Ohio

2nd Printing
© 1991 Susan C. Harriss
All rights reserved.

Published in the United States of America by Cowley Publications, a division of the Society of St. John the Evangelist. No portion of this book may be reproduced, stored in or introduced into a retrieval system, or transmitted, in any form or by any means—including photocopying—without the prior written permission of Cowley Publications, except in the case of brief quotations embodied in critical articles and reviews.

International Standard Book Number: 1-56101-031-6
Library of Congress Number: 90-23649

Library of Congress Cataloging-in-Publication Data
Harriss, Susan C., 1952-
   Jamie's way : stories for worship and family devotion / Susan C. Harriss.
      p. cm.
   Summary: A collection of story-sermons for children about moral and religious questions intended to be read aloud in the context of family worship.
   ISBN 1-56101-031-6 (alk. paper)
   1. Children's sermons. 2. Family—Prayer-books and devotions—English. 3. Children—Prayer books and devotions—English. [1. Sermons. 2. Prayer books and devotions. 3. Christian life.] I. Title.
BV4315.h285 1991
252'.53—dc20   90-23649

This book is printed on acid-free paper and was produced in the United States of America.

The cover illustration is a painting by Augustus John entitled "Portrait of Caspar," printed by permission of the Fitzwilliam Museum in Cambridge, England and Mrs. Vivien White of London.

Cowley Publications
28 Temple Place
Boston, Massachusetts 02111

Forward Movement Publications
412 Sycamore Street
Cincinnati, OH 45202-4195

For Ken

ACKNOWLEDGMENTS

The thanks start at home. Had not my husband listened to the earliest of these stories, and approved and giggled and wept and corrected, there would not have been so many. Our children, Kirsten and Edmund, have listened and cared, too. And since some kinds of work can't be done with even the most adorable children underfoot, I have relied on my friend and helper Allyson Swan to draw them into the next room whenever I needed quiet.

Dan Heischman was the chaplain whose invitation prompted "Jason's Prayer" and so got me started on these stories, while Hays Rockwell made it possible for me to preach regularly to families at St. James Church in New York City. That was a rich five years: my clergy colleagues cheered or winced at the sermons as suited them best, and I thank them for their honesty and love. Ross Tappen typed many of these stories, Barb Shubinski provided feedback, Joan Dunham gave soundings from the back row, and Jane Bryan, surely the world's most experienced Sunday School teacher, cheered me on. Nancy Field listened so intently it was as though she were preaching with me.

In the year since I left St. James, Ann Durrell, Fred Hill, and Patricia Mendenhall have supplied advice and moral support in large doses.

And the kids—at St. James, St. Michael's, at Trinity and Lawrenceville Schools, at St. John's, Kingston—I have to thank them, too. Unprompted praise from a child is heady stuff. Eliot Merrill, Katie Wray, Meredith Draper, Martha Rockwell, Mary Dunham, Laura Hines, Olivia Leon, and more—some of you have grown up already! Thank you.

Last but not least, my editor, Cynthia Shattuck, has my heart for seeing a book in these sermons and for making it real.

TABLE OF CONTENTS

Preface by David H. C. Read   1

Introduction   3

Ways to Use this Book   25

This Little Light   27

Jason's Prayer   33

Janie's Baptism   41

Seeing Is Believing   48

The Blue Watchband Girls   56

Lost and Found   64

A Perfect Gift   72

"And You'll Wear Diamonds"   81

It's the Pits!   91

Almost Persuaded   99

I Want It Now!   108

The Skating Party 119

The Greatest 131

Having It All 140

What Mary Saw 152

A Case of Dread 165

Jamie's Way 173

Never Let Him Go 184

A Saving Grace 193

The Peace of Christ 204

PREFACE
by David H. C. Read

I am unusually impressed by this book in a field that is notoriously difficult and full of traps for the unwary. Susan Harriss has done what some of us have come to regard as impossible: she has created a collection of children's sermons that are neither coy nor boring, neither joky nor condescending, and that are never embarassing to either children or parents.

Her helpful introduction contains a valuable clue to the author's understanding of the art of creating such gems of "junior homiletic." She reveals the theology, psychology, and rich experience that lie behind her stories, as well as a rich imagination and an unusually penetrating access to the mind of children at different ages and from different backgrounds. Susan Harriss avoids the traps of false "relevance" (to use yesterday's slang) and has what I must call theological guts when it comes to content.

These are not little stories with a moral tacked on. The author is not afraid to tackle themes like the Transfiguration, the Passion stories, the Communion of the Saints. Nor does she shy away from situations like divorce, death, cancer, AIDS.

Those of us who have struggled with this art for many years will find this collection of stories both encouraging and corrective. Those who have written off children's sermons as comic relief for a bored congregation or as a hopeless task will be stimulated to rethink their point of view.

I commend this book with enthusiasm and trust it will have a wide circulation, well beyond the specific milieu for which the stories were orginally composed.

David H. C. Read, Minister Emeritus
Madison Avenue Presbyterian Church

INTRODUCTION

The first time somebody asked me to preach to children, I didn't like the idea. I'm not sure why, because I like kids and I'm not a bad preacher. Maybe it was the memory of my own childhood, Sunday mornings with those long lulls at church when you were supposed to keep quiet no matter what. Somehow preaching to children sounded like a non sequitur; you couldn't honestly preach to children, you could only bore them. Otherwise you were only entertaining them, which isn't the same as preaching.

But the invitation came from a friend, a chaplain at a private school. He needed someone to speak at the lower school chapel, and I didn't think I should refuse. Still I worried about making the kids restless, about annoying their teachers (I imagined that a poorly run assembly could ruin a teacher's whole day), about disappointing Dan, who had invited me. I said yes, but I also said a little prayer: "Dear God, just don't let me be boring."

Not long after that my husband and I indulged ourselves and bought a video game; they had just come on the market, and we were delighted with our new toy. I found myself daydreaming about video games, and imagined a little boy who wanted God to get him a Pacman game just like mine. Of course! He had heard that passage from the Bible, "Seek and ye shall find, knock and the door shall be opened to you...." He would naturally think God would give him the game! Like a crochet square the idea grew and grew until this little boy had a mother, a father, a grouchy brother, and a Sunday school lesson. I had my sermon! It was "Jason's Prayer."

When the day of the chapel service came I was excited. I was going to give these kids a pleasant surprise: a story instead of a sermon! And they loved it. I liked the story, too; I liked Jason, I liked Pacman, and I liked all the walks and places I had added to the story to make it work. Most of all it

INTRODUCTION

gave me a way to like those squirming kids—I felt like one of them.

It was four years later before I got a chance to preach to children in a parish church. At St. James' Episcopal Church in New York City, the Sunday family service was well attended and planned to include children in every part of the liturgy. On communion Sundays, children aged six and up stayed with their parents till the service ended. "Preach in a way that somehow includes the children," the planning group told me as I prepared my first sermon there, "but don't leave out the adults."

That was a challenge, a kind of double jeopardy. Here was a chance to bore the kids and annoy their parents, too, giving them what my husband calls a "sweaty experience." If I couldn't persuade the children to listen, or at least sit still, all of their parents would be too busy shushing and holding, glaring and warning, to hear any of the sermon.

I looked at the gospel reading for the day and groaned. It was the parable of the feast, the feast where none of the guests show up.

The host gets mad, and invites anyone who will come—beggars, street people, anybody. The parable ends with some scary business about the one guest who came in without the proper clothes; he gets thrown out into utter darkness! Definitely not G-rated, that gospel. Not one of your "fun" passages. What was I going to do? This time it wasn't just a question of not being boring, it was a question of making sense. How could you make sense of this parable to kids, and not scare them out of their wits? How could you keep them from fixing on the guest with the wrong clothes at the end of the story? (Can't you just see it? Some poor kid who came in without a tie breaks into a sweat. What will God do to him?) What about that mean host, that tough-minded God? How could I preach that gospel to kids?

As it happened, I had a new watchband that year—an embroidered ribbon watchband. Another St. James' priest had a watchband like it, although his had lobsters embroidered on it, and mine had strawberries. Somehow the two watchbands and my anxiety about the sermon came together in

INTRODUCTION

my mind and Genevieve Moreau appeared, a little girl who wanted to be in with the popular girls in her school, in with a clique known as as the "Blue Watchband Girls." I told Genevieve's story, adding a few comments about the Scripture at the end, and it was just fine.

After that I rarely faced the congregation without a story. I tried several times to go back to expository preaching, but it just didn't make sense. The kids liked the sermons; their Sunday School teachers reported that they talked about them later in their classes. Their parents were grateful. They said things like, "He sat still!" and "She was on the edge of her seat!" and "She actually listens when you preach." And they were relieved that they didn't have to work so hard at controlling their kids during the sermon. Some parents would surely have liked something more challenging to them intellectually. But the children never seemed to tire of the stories, and a surprising number of adults confided, almost sheepishly, that they liked the stories, too.

They understood them; they felt nourished by them; they were hearing the gospel.

And the children never suggested that I was doing something different from my colleagues, who still preached in the expository style at these services. They just said, "I liked your sermon," or better, "I understood your sermon." They didn't call them stories at all. They understood that I was preaching to them.

My style developed. I preached from the chancel steps, where I could be nearer to the people. I started enclosing the sermons in a large notebook, resting the book on a music stand so that my hands were free. I ad-libbed here and there. I started watching faces, filling in gaps where they didn't seem to be getting the point, trying for the occasional laugh.

Meanwhile my first child was getting old enough to be asking for stories of her own. I tried things out on her, practicing and playing. I listened to the stories my husband told her, too. Listening to his stories helped almost as much as the comments he made on my stories; he had such great ideas! The

INTRODUCTION

more stories I wrote, the more came to me. I studied the Bible passage first, then set it aside and let my imagination work. As I grew more confident about the stories, I began to say less about the Scripture passage itself. Sometimes I simply read it at the beginning and end of the story. The stories *became* the commentary; they were the sermons.

Pastoral problems made their way into the sermons. Some weeks after a savage attack on a young woman in Central Park, I found myself writing the park scene in "The Peace of Christ." In "Jamie's Way," about a rich girl in a city hospital, I hoped to show some very rich children that they could act like Christians, too. In "Having It All," I was working on the problem of materialism. More and more I found that problems like these could be addressed within the narratives themselves; I didn't need to isolate them or talk about them in the abstract. When I *did* talk in the abstract, even about important things like suffering, endurance, even about grace, the vitality began to escape from the sermons like air from a leaky tire. More and more I could see the wisdom of the writing teacher's edict, "Don't tell me—show me!"

Clearly, the story was the thing. But why? How could I be sure I wasn't merely entertaining them, and not conveying the gospel at all? Was the story just a convenient form for me to use, or was it the best way to talk to children about the faith? Maybe it wasn't a coincidence that Jesus did so much of his teaching in stories, those pithy, knotty parables in the gospels. Why would stories be the better way to preach, especially to children?

In thinking these questions through, I went back to the theories of Jean Piaget, the famous child psychologist. His work, though difficult to digest, has made a great impact on the ways in which western children are reared and taught. Piaget has shifted our thinking about children and their education from *what* they know to *how* they know, how they think. Children are not just ignorant adults, lacking in information. If that were so, you could just

INTRODUCTION

tell them what they need to know and be sure they memorized it all on time.

But Piaget's research suggests that children don't think the same way adults do at all. They literally manage ideas differently in their minds. In fact children may not think at all, at least not in the sense of managing ideas—abstract concepts—until they reach adolescence, or the stage that Piaget called formal operations. They don't think about "life," they think about the day, or maybe just the moment at hand.

This is why the typical Sunday sermon is so dry for them. Let's say I wanted to preach on the Beatitudes, or just one beatitude: "Blessed are the meek." For an adult I would brainstorm about the passage, and develop a talk about humility and its importance in the Christian life, true versus false humility, and so on. I would probably talk a bit about the conflict between being meek and looking out for yourself, the problem many Christians have with asserting themselves while taking the gospel seriously. You get the idea. This sermon could be fine for adults, but it would bore their children to tears.

This isn't because children don't know about humility. Absolutely not! They know a lot about it! It takes up a part of every day for them: humility or the lack of it on the playground, picking teams, comparing skills. ("Hey, Joey, look at this! I can hit the ball to the edge of the field! You can't even bunt yet!") Given the right sort of questioning your average school-aged kid could come up with examples of humility—or the lack thereof—and tell you a few stories about it. But you couldn't just say, "Tell me what you think of humility as a virtue." You would have to show the child what you mean. This is because for the school-aged child the concept is trapped in the experience. Children know all too well about humility. But they would be unable to isolate the virtue from their experience of it; they can tell you the story in which humility figures, but they cannot isolate the quality of humility itself and talk about it apart from a concrete situation. They can

INTRODUCTION

tell you the story, and the story is their way of "knowing" about this idea, humility.

This ability to "narratize" experience, to arrange events in sequence and talk about them, is part of Piaget's stage of concrete operations. It is an ability developed in the early school years, beginning at age six or seven. Younger children, ages three to six, cannot manage it. They can hear stories and absorb them, but they cannot repeat them in a way that makes sense to the rest of us. Have you ever asked a five-year-old to tell you about a movie? You will be listening for days. No concept of time, or order: "And then this happened, and that happened, and this happened." The events won't seem to make up any coherent pattern. The only thing you'll be sure about is that this kid likes to talk! But an older child can hear the story and tell it. This sets him apart from his younger siblings; his inability to talk about the concepts in the story sets him apart from his older ones. But all children, even tiny ones, enjoy stories and will listen to them, whether they can repeat them or not.

The wonderful news in this for preachers is that children learn about concepts through stories. This means that we can communicate with them in a meaningful way about the love of God, about patience, about God's nature, about sacrifice—about almost anything. And this is a two-way street: young Janey can discuss the virtue of humility by telling stories about it, and she can learn about humility by hearing stories about it. The concept is trapped in the experience, like a rabbit in a thicket; if she could take the thicket home, she could have it. It's very near to her, you see; she knows about it; she just can't capture it without its context. But we can put the context back and talk about it, and she understands.

Once we realise this, we can talk to children about very deep things indeed. We can have a soul talk with them, and they just might tell us some amazing things. It may be that school-aged children, and maybe even younger children, too, have experiences of God that they don't or can't talk about. Maybe it makes them feel awkward, or unusual. They don't hear their parents talking about such things. Does this mean their parents don't pray, or have experiences with God? Does this mean that God is something We Don't Talk About?

In the intensely evangelical sect where I was raised, altar calls ended every Sunday morning service, and big regional meetings for young people were held every year. Children were taught to pray very early on. We had family devotions most nights, and I "accepted Christ" in a conscious way when I was seven. Even in this atmosphere, thick with religion, my parents kept their spiritual business to themselves, and rarely if ever asked me about mine. I just assumed that my faith was like their faith, only younger.

When I was ten I went to one of these regional youth meetings with my parents. I was under age for this meeting but was allowed to go because they needed a child my age for a play called "The Man Who Loved Children." The morning after the play there was a longish prayer meeting, with lots of singing and praying and a prolonged altar call. The speaker kept inviting anybody who "wanted to get right with God" to "come forward" to the altar, to kneel there and pray. I was familiar with all this, and wanted very much to go. I had been having a hard year at school—not making friends, really, and feeling out of place much of the time in the rural town to which my parents had just moved. And I had built up that play in my imagination as the thing that would show everybody how talented I was. In fact the play was short, the part was small, and I was only so-so in my part as the child who came to Jesus. In the course of this altar call it occurred to me that I needed what that preacher was talking about; I had already accepted Christ, as they said, but now they were asking for people who felt they needed help with their lives, and that description fit me perfectly.

So I went up and knelt. A nice lady who had helped with the play came and knelt beside me, and said, "Dear little Susan, do you want to be friends with the man who loves children?"

INTRODUCTION

I nodded compliantly, but inside I was shocked. I was already friends with Jesus, I was sure of that. Was she implying that I had to start over? Was there something wrong with me? Was I old beyond my years to think that I already had a prayer life, that I could go up to that altar and settle accounts the way the grown-ups did? It had never occurred to me that I might be too young for the salvation they were preaching.

Of course the irony of all this is that the play was supposed to be about Jesus' loving children, yet there was only one part for a child in it. (How like the church!) Jesus himself made the point that children were welcome to come to him, and not for any of the reasons one might choose: because they were cute, or needed tending, or because he needed to endear himself to their parents. They were welcome because "of such is the Kingdom of Heaven."

What I couldn't convey to that lady was that I had already accepted everything the preacher had said and was raring to go. I knew, at least at that moment I knew, that I loved God more than anything or anyone else in the world, and I wanted to do something about it. But she seemed to think it would all be new to me. I was embarrassed, even angry, and felt more alone than before.

In *Returning, A Spiritual Journey*, Dan Wakefield relates an experience he had as a boy, an experience that demonstrates some of the same qualities.

> On an ordinary school night I went to bed, turned out the light, said the Lord's Prayer, as I always did and prepared to go to sleep. I lay there only a few moments, not long enough to go to sleep (I was clearly and vividly awake during this whole experience) when I had the sensation that my whole body was filled with light. It was a white light of such brightness and intensity that it seemed almost silver. It was neither hot nor cold, neither burning nor soothing, it was simply there, filling every part of my body from my head to my feet. I did not hear any voice, or any sound at all for that matter, but with the light came the understanding that it was Christ. The light was the presence of Christ, and I was not simply in his presence, his presence was in me.

> ...I don't think I told anyone about it, at least not for some years. I didn't need to ask anyone about it, because I so clearly knew what it was, and I didn't want to try to explain to others who, not having had the experience, would not be able to understand (pp. 39-40).

The contexts for the two experiences are very different: mine in an evangelical meeting, his at home; and my experience was not so much finding God as being surprised to know that others assumed I hadn't, or couldn't. But Wakefield and I shared, at that young age, a kind of certainty about God, one that was short-lived and yet has influenced us long after.

Who knows what other children are seeing God, or hearing Him, or simply looking in a serious way? And aren't their lives hard enough to warrant some help from heaven? Surely we can give them the benefit of the doubt: spiritual experience begins when you have it, not when you come of age. As a pastor I think parents and preachers ought to know this; just because the kids are wriggling and giggling in church doesn't mean they're not absorbing anything. They take in more than we can know.

This is not to say that all school-aged children are introspective, thinking about God all the time. In fact their absorption with concrete operations (Piaget's term) may make them doubtful, even scornful, of religious teaching. "Ah," a parent might say, "my kids aren't like Dan Wakefield. They just want the facts!" And they're right. The little empiricists, kids from six to eleven, are the ones asking, "Did that really happen?" They are busy sorting out Santa Claus and the Tooth Fairy, and may be quite ready to "sort out" the Resurrection, too, and consign it to the world of make believe. They want proof. "Show me! Explain to me!" is their incessant cry. They may have been wildly playful and imaginative at four or five, but now they've set that aside for more important things.

It's tough going for parents at this age; how long can the Tooth Fairy sneak around and not be discovered? And of course they will be put on the spot regularly, right along with the Sunday School teachers, about

INTRODUCTION

whether the Bible is true. "Did this really happen?" they ask over and over again. With an adult you might want to move into a discussion of the nature of truth: "It's not that there were two carpenter ants in the ark, but the point that all creation was represented...." With kids you can't do that. They won't get it; they'll think that you are bluffing. (So will some adults, but that's another subject.)

With these young empiricists the story gives you an alternative way of speaking. Rather than try to explain the Bible, or prove it, the story says, "I believe what the Bible says happened. Let me show you a way that it could happen." The children know that you are just telling a story, and yet you're also showing them how something might just be possible. This goes for the miracle stories as well as for the sayings of Jesus. You can take an everyday experience that has a bit of wonder in it, and show them that wonderful things are true. "Let's think of a way the Transfiguration might have happened," the story says, "let's pretend it happened to someone you know, and you were there." We try this way to give the child the experience directly, without fussing about what is true, or how it is true, or what it means. You respect their intelligence; they can sort it out for themselves later on, or better yet, leave the question open. The story leaves it up to them.

Many of the sermons presented in this collection present children who are having spiritual adventures of their own: some in dreams, some at the Eucharist, some in that borderland between prayer and the imagination. Some of the characters are acting like Christ, others feel His love through the mediation of loving adults. One, the suicidal teenager in "A Saving Grace," meets God face to face. The stories are realistic, up to a point; in many, the supernatural intrudes in a natural setting. Only one, "This Little Light," takes place entirely in the realm of fantasy. The other settings are loosely drawn copies of the communities in which they were preached. They use everyday objects and feelings and experiences,

INTRODUCTION

just as Jesus' parables used the vineyards, sheepfolds, and fishing tackle of his time. All of this takes a great risk. The risk is believing that God actually speaks to children, that God cares about what they do and who they are—not just whether they are sick or well, or whether they obey their parents. The claim is that the soul's conversation with God begins long before what we call adulthood, before the "age of reason," before confirmation. It begins well before children have learned to sit still, to behave in church, or to recite the creed. And if the conversation has already begun, then we preachers, and parents, have only to acknowledge it. And admire it.

"Suffer the children to come unto me, for of such is the Kingdom of Heaven." Are these young Christians seeing more of God than we know? So much of living asks them to forget what they have seen! Perhaps all we can do at church is give them permission to remember, to claim aloud or in their hearts, that God is real to them now. Heaven can wait, but it needn't. "Little ones to Him belong."

WAYS TO USE THIS BOOK

The stories in this book are arranged roughly in order of difficulty. The stories at the front of the book are suitable for younger children; the stories at the back are for adolescents. Always look over the story before reading it aloud; you'll give a more expressive reading, and not be caught off guard by surprises, or subjects that might be troublesome for your children. Here are some suggestions for using this book.

FOR DEVOTIONS AT HOME

Families can use the stories for devotions. Pick a quiet time and place, and allow about half an hour. Invite an older child to read the Bible passage first. Then read the story as dramatically as you like; take some time to talk about the story, using the questions provided as a starting point. Finish with a short prayer—a reading child might like to lead the one provided in the book—

and any other prayers you like to use together.

Like any other children's activity, this improves with repetition. Using the same place and time—a favorite spot on the sofa, or around the table after dinner—will help younger children settle in, and know what to expect. Try different ways until you find a routine that suits you.

FOR SCHOOL AND CHILDREN'S CHAPEL

All of these stories were written to be read aloud in some sort of worship service, and they can be used that way again. Just be sure that the Scripture passage provided is read clearly and audibly beforehand, just before the story itself.

FOR OLDER CHILDREN, ON THEIR OWN

Older school children and teens may prefer to have the stories in their own possession, and some will be more meaningful if read in private. ("A Saving Grace," which deals with teen suicide, is one.) You might give the book to confirmation students as a gift or a supplement to what they read at church.

*T*HIS LITTLE LIGHT

"You are the light of the world. A city built on a hill cannot be hid. No one after lighting a lamp puts it under the bushel basket, but on the lampstand, and it gives light to all in the house. In the same way, let your light so shine before others, so that they may see your good works and give glory to your Father in heaven." Matthew 5:14-16

In the land of the grubs, a terrible darkness fell. Not all at once, mind you, but a little at a time. It fell so softly, so gradually, that by the time it was completely dark all the grubs had adjusted to it. They had just enough light to move around, but not enough to read by; enough to get to work, but not enough to see the smile on another grub's face. Softly and slowly it fell, this darkness, gently, and in a friendly sort of way. And so although the grubs could not see one another, although they had always to move slowly to keep from falling, although they only reached out into that darkness to keep from bumping into one another, the grubs accepted the darkness. "Dark is the way things are," they said. "Life is dark." And, "The dark you have always with you."

It really was quite terribly dark! But they didn't care. They had accepted it.

Until one day Johnny, the smallest and very nearly the youngest of the grubs—oh, I'd say he was only six or so—made a powerful discovery. Johnny found some light. Not in his pocket, not in the old flashlight in the kitchen drawer, and not on a lamp. He found the light in himself. He *was* the light.

Here's how it happened: he started looking up.

It was by accident, really, he was just stretching, but he started to look up to see what was there. The sky. He was looking up, and squinting, thinking, Maybe it isn't black all the way up—maybe there's something up there I can see if I look hard enough....And the next thing you knew, his chest began to glow. He looked down at his chest just in time to see it, but then it began to fade. When he looked up it was bright; when he looked down it grew dim. How about that? he thought, and went to find his friend Simon. "Simon," he said, "Look at this. I've got a light!"

"Where, in your pocket?" Simon wanted to know.

"No, right here," he said. "Watch me!"

And he lifted up his head, and opened his eyes wide, to look as hard as he could at the sky.

"Hey, let me see that!" Simon said and reached out to touch Johnny's chest. He touched the light, and as he did, he, Simon, began to glow a bit himself. "That's amazing!" they said. And went to find their friends.

So they went to find Rebecca, and Samuel, and Jenny, and some of the other little grubs they knew. They went out into a field, deep in one of the old parks where no one played any more (because it was too dark, of course) and they tried to find ways to make the light shine.

Here are some of the things that worked: singing, holding hands, sharing toys, touching kindly, sharing food. And saying the old rhymes they knew, rhymes no one bothered with much any more, rhymes about the light.

They went and found other young grubs to help them. The ones who were sick, they carried to the park. The ones who were afraid, they helped along. The ones who were angry with their brothers and sisters, the ones who were crying, they persuaded to come anyway. "You can be angry later," they told them. "Just come see this."

And so the grubs arrived in the field in the center of the park. By now some of them had been touching so much and sharing so much and singing so much that they glowed all the time. But they wanted to make the light shine even more, they wanted their moms and dads to see it; they wanted to see enough light to read by, and to see each other's smiles by; they wanted enough light for the park to be safe again.

And so they made a circle, a circle hundreds of grubs around. They joined hands, they began to sing, and they looked up. They all looked up at once and the light was stupendous. There was so much light someone remembered what that kind of

THIS LITTLE LIGHT

light was called. "Hey, it's daylight!" she cried. And so it was.

But still they looked up. And saw there, in the sky above them, a large and kindly face. It was the father of light, and He was smiling.

And in the land of the grubs, some ways off, the older grubs looked up themselves and saw. What they saw was light, but not light only; what they saw most was the smiling face in the sky above them.

"My goodness," they said to one another. "Look at that! I thought someone was watching, but I didn't want to say anything." And as they looked up, of course, the light around them grew greater still.

"You are the light of the world," Jesus said. "Let your light shine enough so that others will see what you do, and know that God is great."

Let your little light shine.

THINGS TO THINK ABOUT

Have you ever been somewhere that was really dark? Were you outdoors or indoors? What was it like? How did you feel?

If you were caught in a dark place like that today, what would you do for light?

What kinds of things did the grubs in the story do to make the light shine more? Can you think of any they didn't try that might have worked?

Jesus told his followers, "You are the light of the world." What do you think he meant?

PRAYING TOGETHER

Close your eyes for just a minute and think of one thing you might do that is kind, and imagine yourself doing that kind thing. Now imagine that while you do that kind thing, you are full of light!

"Lord Jesus, thank you for giving us the light of your love. Help us to let our lights shine. Amen."

*J*ASON'S PRAYER

"Ask, and it will be given you; search, and you will find; knock, and the door will be opened for you. For everyone who asks receives, and everyone who searches finds, and for everyone who knocks, the door will be opened. Is there anyone among you who, if your child asks for bread, will give a stone? Or if the child asks for a fish, will give a snake? If you then, who are evil, know how to give good gifts to your children, how much more will your Father in heaven give good things to those who ask him!" Matthew 7:7-11

Things just weren't going Jason's way that Sunday morning. He had a fight with Eddie, his older brother, before breakfast. His father made him eat oatmeal, which he hated, and then he had to put on a coat and tie for Sunday School. He really was tired of putting on a coat and tie for anything, so after his dad made the knot in the tie Jason yanked at it and started yelling and running all over the apartment. That made his father mad; it also made his mother, who was sleeping late that day, yell at him from the bedroom.

By the time they got to church his shirt was already untucked, and he suddenly realized he hadn't remembered to wash his hands after he crawled under the bed looking for his shoes. He took a quick look at his hands. "Phew!" he whistled. "Pretty dirty!" So he stuck his hands into his pants pockets, which made his shirt come even more untucked. He looked a mess.

At least they got to Sunday School on time. He and Eddie were in different classes, so he wouldn't have to worry about his older brother bugging him. He was relieved about that. He got to his classroom, took a seat in the corner, pushed his hands further into his pockets, and stared at the floor.

For a moment he thought he was going to cry. He slunk lower in his chair—so low he had to wrap his ankles around the legs to keep from sliding out. "Dumb, Jason," he said to himself. "Real dumb. Just start thinking about something else."

The teacher came in and led the class in the opening song; they recited the creed and took the offering. Jason said all the words but somehow he wasn't really there. He was thinking about Pacman—the video game.

He loved to play it. This little round guy could eat up all the stuff on the screen—big dots and red monster things—and if you played really well it made great noises. Jason was good at it. He was the best of all his school friends, except for Joey Daniels. That was because Joey had a Pacman at his house. And of course he wasn't as good as Eddie, but Eddie was older, so he didn't count.

All of a sudden Jason got a great idea. His birthday was coming. Wouldn't it be neat if he got a Pacman game for his birthday? Then he could practice and beat Joey Daniels! Maybe he could even beat Eddie! He started thinking, thinking hard, so hard that his face got red. The next thing you know Miss Andrews, the teacher, was looking right at him, and asking, "Jason, are you feeling all right? You're awfully quiet today."

"Uh, yes, Miss Andrews. I'm all right."

"Well how about reading to us from the New Testament, then?"

"Yes, ma'am." He got up, his hands still in his pockets, and shuffled to the front of the room. She handed him a big black Bible and pointed to these words: "Ask and you will receive."

"Start here," she said.

So Jason started at Matthew 7:7.

"Ask and you will receive; seek and you will find; knock and the door will be opened to you. For everyone who asks receives, he who seeks finds, and to him who knocks, the door will be opened."

Jason went back to his chair. Now he had an even better idea. "Ask and you will receive—isn't that what it said?" he thought. He bit his lower lip and closed one eye—maybe he could pray without Miss Andrews noticing. "Dear God. Please, pleeeease, pul-l-ease let me get a Pacman for my birthday! Amen."

Miss Andrews passed out paper for them to draw pictures, and you can guess what Jason drew: it was the playing surface of a Pacman game.

After Sunday School Jason asked his father and Eddie to wait for him while he went to the bathroom. Only he didn't go to the bathroom. Instead he ran over to the side chapel in the church — he almost knocked Mrs. Baum over on his way. He went in and stood right at the front, facing the altar. He looked at the flowers, the big brass cross, and the candlesticks. Then he closed his eyes and got ready to pray. It was quiet except for the sound of people going out the back of the church. So Jason said to himself, "Okay, concentrate." He tried to think about God, and he tried to think about Pacman.

Something went wrong, though. Every time he tried to think about God, he thought instead about Eddie and the fight they'd had that morning. He remembered how mad he had been with his father about the tie. He could almost see his father's face getting red, could hear his mother shouting from the bedroom. It didn't feel like praying, so far. So finally he said this—very quietly, because he was a bit embarrassed: "Dear God, I didn't like this morning very much, you probably know that I didn't want to come to Sunday School. I really hated Eddie, and I don't like to wear a tie. If I was dumb, please forgive me. I really would like to have a Pacman for my birthday."

He was about to say Amen, but added this: "Oh, but if I don't get Pacman, I guess that's okay, too."

Jason opened one eye, and saw the flower to the left of the cross. Was he dreaming? It looked bigger than before. Pinker, too. He opened both eyes, wide, then shrugged, and said Amen. He turned to go.

He was surprised to see his father and Eddie waiting for him at the back of the chapel. As they left, Eddie said, "Hey Jace! That's some bathroom!" and his father said, "I think it's fine that you went to the chapel, Jason—you didn't have to make up that business about the bathroom."

That afternoon Jason and his father went to Central Park to watch the toy sailboats on the little pond. It was a perfect day for it—a blue sky, a little breeze, and just enough sun so you could be comfortable without a jacket. It was Jason's favorite place in the park. He and his father stood watching the boats, both of them with their hands in their pockets.

"Jason—" his father began. He was still looking at the water, so Jason knew he was thinking. "Were you praying in the chapel this morning?"

"Sure, Dad," Jason answered.

"May I ask about what? You don't have to tell me."

"Well, we read in Sunday School about how you can ask God for stuff, so I went in to ask God to get me Pacman for my birthday."

"Did you ask Him?"

"Sort of. But mainly I just ended up talking to Him, and being quiet. It felt funny."

"Bad funny?"

"No, good funny, like everything was going to be all right."

"Hmm," his dad said. They stood a moment without speaking. "Did God say anything about Pacman?"

"Gee, I don't know..." Jason thought, and remembered the moment when he opened one eye, and saw that big pink flower beside the cross. "I think He said what you said."

"Oh? What's that?"

"'We'll see!'"

JAMIE'S WAY

Jason laughed, and his father laughed and chucked him under the chin. He looked at him, and Jason could see that his father was pleased. "Yep, Jason, we'll see."

The flowers around the pond seemed big and bright as Jason took his father's hand and pulled him, laughing, toward the path for home.

THINGS TO THINK ABOUT

Have you ever wanted something badly, something that you weren't likely to get?

Did you ask God to give it to you? What happened?

Did you feel that God had answered your prayer? Why, or why not? What can we do if we feel disappointed about not getting something we want?

PRAYING TOGETHER

Remember the last time you asked God for something, and what happened.

"Dear God, thank you for hearing our prayers when we ask for things. Help us to understand when we can't have what we ask. Amen."

*J*ANIE'S BAPTISM

People were bringing little children to him in order that he might touch them; and the disciples spoke sternly to them. But when Jesus sae this, he was indignant and said to them, "Let the little children come to me; do not stop them; for it is to such as these that the kingdom of God belongs. Truly I tell you, whoever does not receive the kingdom of God as a little child will never enter it." And he took them up in his arms and blessed them. Mark 10:13-16

You are sealed by the Holy Spirit in Baptism and marked as Christ's own for ever. The Book of Common Prayer

Janie Blake was worried about all this baptism business. It seemed so serious to her, and so confusing. Janie was six years old, and she was only now getting baptized. At the church they usually baptized babies. But Janie's Mom and Dad grew up in another church where you didn't get baptized until you were grown up. Or at least eleven. So they thought Janie should wait until she was old enough to understand what was happening to her. Old enough to know what she was doing.

Only Janie wasn't sure she knew.

When she was little she thought getting baptized was like getting a shot at the doctor's office, sort of like getting vaccinated. Maybe it was like getting a shot to keep you from getting sick. But that turned out not to be true: it wasn't a shot, it didn't hurt, and it wouldn't keep you from getting sick. In fact Patty Alston's baby brother got sick on the day he was baptized. So it certainly wouldn't keep you from getting sick.

Janie's Sunday School teacher said getting baptized was like being washed, or taking a bath. But Janie didn't feel dirty. And besides she could take a bath at home any time she wanted. Then the teacher said it was supposed to wash away sin. But if sin was something you did wrong, what good would taking a bath do? Once when she was four Janie got chocolate pudding all over the kitchen floor. Her mother had told her not even to touch the pudding until after dinner, but Janie had disobeyed, and made a terrible mess. She didn't think her mother would find out, because she cleaned up all the pudding she could see. She had washed everything! Her face, her hands, the floor.

JANIE'S BAPTISM

But her mother still found out, and she got punished anyway. So Janie didn't see how washing could take away bad things that you did. It sure didn't help when she got in trouble over the pudding! But then her Sunday School teacher said baptism was like a bath for your soul; it made you feel clean and new inside the way a bath made you feel clean and new on the outside. Janie liked that idea. She liked playing with bubbles in the tub, and making the soap all lathery amd smooth, and then rinsing away every single speck of soap and dirt. When her mother washed her hair she rubbed her hair together with her fingers at the end. If it squeaked, she said, "Now that's what I call clean!" So if baptism was that kind of bath, maybe that was okay.

But what if she had to take her clothes off in church? When her mother told her she was getting a new white dress for the baptism, that made Janie feel better. Janie asked if she could keep the dress on the whole time, and her mother looked puzzled. "Of course!" she said. "What did you think?" Janie didn't answer her. Just as long as she didn't have to get undressed, she figured it would be all right.

When the day came to practice for the baptism Janie went to church with her parents, and their minister explained more about what would happen on the day of the baptism. He said he was going to mark her forehead with the sign of the cross so that she would be marked as Christ's own forever, just as it said in her Prayer Book. But she looked on the table in the church, and there was no marker. She thought he might use a magic marker—or maybe ashes, the way they did at church on Ash Wednesday. Maybe it would be magic ink that glowed in the dark. She hoped so; that would be neat. Or maybe it was some invisible ink that only God could see. The minister said that was almost true—not the part about the ink, exactly, but the part about God seeing her.

He said baptism made her a Christian, and God would always be able to see her and know where she was. God had always known about her and cared for her, but now it would be different. Now she would belong to Jesus in a very special way. He told her that Jesus loved her very much, and would always be her friend, no matter what happened. And he taught her a song to help her remember:

> Now I belong to Jesus.
> Jesus belongs to me.
> Not for the years of time alone
> But for eternity.

The minister told her that even Jesus got baptized, in the Jordan River. That made her feel better about it. Jesus got baptized, too. She wondered if Jesus had been worried, like her.

Finally Sunday came. Janie put on her new white dress, and new white shoes. And even though her mother said she didn't need white gloves, she wore them anyway, because they made her feel special.

The minister baptized the babies first, and then Janie. She stood beside the gleaming silver bowl and put her head down. The minister splashed her forehead three times. The water was cool. Her bangs got wet. He gave her a little towel to dry her face. Then he put his thumb into a little silver jar, and dabbed the oil on her forehead, making the sign of the cross. And it didn't hurt a bit. In fact, she wasn't even thinking about whether it hurt or not, she was thinking: "Now I belong to Jesus. Now I belong to Jesus." And caught her mother's eye, who looked so proud. And took her father's hand. And inside, yes, she did feel shiny and new. Shiny as her new white shoes.

The next thing she knew it was over. The minister was saying, "The peace of the Lord be always with you." And for just that moment she knew, she absolutely knew, what that peace was about.

THINGS TO THINK ABOUT

Have you been baptized? Do you remember it? Did it happen when you were a baby, or much later?

Can you think of some reasons why parents might wait and have their children baptized later, the way Janie's parents did? Do you know anyone who was baptized later?

JANIE'S BAPTISM

What do you think it means to be "marked as Christ's own forever?" Why do you think that might be a good thing?

Once you're baptized, does it mean that you can never do anything wrong again? What happens if you do?

PRAYING TOGETHER

Take a minute to think about being fresh, clean and new, like a clean sheet of paper ready for a picture.

"Lord Jesus, thank you for making us your friends in baptism. Help us whenever we get into trouble to ask for your help so that we can be fresh and new again, just the way Janie felt when she was baptized. Amen."

Seeing is Believing

But Thomas (who was called the Twin), one of the twelve, was not with them when Jesus came. So the other disciples told him, "We have seen the Lord." But he said to them, "Unless I see the mark of the nails in his hands, and put my finger in the mark of the nails and put my hand in his side, I will not believe."

A week later his disciples were again in the house, and Thomas was with them. Although the doors were shut, Jesus came and stood among them and said, "Peace be with you." Then he said to Thomas, "Put your finger here and see my hands. Reach out your hand and put it in my side. Do not doubt, but believe." Thomas answered him, "My Lord and my God!" Jesus said to him, "Have you believed because you have seen me? Blessed are those who have not seen and yet have come to believe." John 20:24-29

When Kathy Thomas woke up Saturday morning the first thing she did was yell for her Dad. This was the day he'd be back from his trip!

She hadn't seen him in three days; he'd been on a business trip to Syracuse. He was supposed to get home very late the night before, well after she and her younger sister had gone to bed. But before he'd left for Syracuse he'd promised that on Saturday, they

SEEING IS BELIEVING

would do something special together, and Kathy had all kinds of ideas about what that ought to be.

She sat up in bed and yelled "Da-a-ad!" No answer. Maybe he was sleeping in. She got up, she put on her robe, and went down the hall to her parents' bedroom. Empty bed. At least he was up. She checked the living room. Not there. None of the bathroom doors were closed; he wouldn't be there. She went and found her mother in the kitchen.

"Where the heck is Dad?" she asked her mother. "I thought he was coming in last night."

"He did come back," her mother said. "He's just gone out to the store. See, his running jacket's gone from the hook."

She looked and saw that her mother was right. Her Dad always wore the same red jacket to run errands around the house on the weekend, and that jacket was missing from the hook. Kathy looked a little bit further: his briefcase was in the foyer, the newspaper was folded in half the long way, and on the kitchen table, right at his place, there was a half-drunk cup of black coffee.

He was home all right. She knew all the signs. She hadn't seen him, but she could tell from the briefcase, the empty hook, and the half-drunk cup of coffee on the table, that he was back. Besides that, her mother had told her. She didn't have any reason to doubt her mother. Her dad was home and would be back any minute. She had seen all she needed to see.

A few minutes later, two-year-old Lindsay woke up. She was harder to convince. Little Lindsay came padding down the hallway into the kitchen calling "Daddy! Where's my Daddy?" When she didn't see him she was inconsolable. Her mother picked her up. "Daddy was just here!" she said, reassuringly. "Daddy will be right back."

But Lindsay wasn't convinced. She wouldn't stop crying. "Daddy not home," she kept saying. "Daddy not home."

Kathy got up from the table thinking she could help. She said, "Look, Baby, here's his briefcase. He brought it in last night. And look, here's the cup of coffee he was just drinking—he has to be here. And look—who else folds the newspaper this way?" Lindsay stopped crying for about thirty seconds, just long enough to think about it, and then her face crumpled into tears again. She still wasn't satisfied. Kathy looked at her mother, who was leaning on the sink and shaking her head.

"You have to see it to believe it, don't you, Lindsay?"

Just then they heard the elevator open in the hallway, and shut; then front door of their apartment open and shut. Sure enough, there was Dad. Lindsay ran into the hall. He scooped her up in one arm, and Kathy in the other, and gave both girls a hug.

It still took Lindsay a few minutes to settle down. She had to see it, and she had to get that hug. In fact, before he even got back to his cup of coffee she wanted to know what he'd brought her from Syracuse.

Now when Jesus came back from the dead, his disciples saw him. All but Thomas. And they told Thomas that Jesus was back, and that they'd actually seen him, and they were glad about it. So there were a lot of signs that something special had happened. But Thomas wasn't satisfied. He said, "Until I see Him, until I put my hand in the wounds, I'm not going to believe it." Thomas wanted to touch the wounds from the crucifixion; he wasn't going to believe it until he saw it with his own eyes, and actually touched Jesus.

But there were other ways to know that Jesus had come back, just the way Kathy knew, once she checked it out, all the signs that her Dad was home.

In the case of Kathy and Lindsay you could say, well, it's just because Kathy's older. Kathy can figure that out. She's had the experience, and she knows the signs: she knows her Dad comes back. Lindsay just hasn't had time to figure all that out yet.

It may have been that way with the disciples. Some of them saw, and understood. They got it right away. Thomas needed more convincing. He had to see Jesus with his own eyes. And he wanted to put his hands in Jesus' wounds.... And the rest of us—well, we have to believe it by hearing it, hearing it from other people. And we have to believe the way Kathy figured out that her Dad was home: by checking out the signs that Jesus Christ is really risen.

We do it by noticing the signs that he's been around. That he's been back, so to speak, causing people to be kind, helping people to forgive one another; maybe answering our prayers, helping sick people to get well, keeping the promises he made, just as Kathy and Lindsay's father kept his promise to them.

But Jesus said, after he saw Thomas, "Blessed are they who have not seen, and yet have believed." The ones who have not seen: that's us. None of us has stood in the same room with the physical body of the risen Christ, or had the chance to touch his wounds. Nobody for nineteen hundred and fifty some years has had the opportunity to stand in that room and say, "I'm not going to believe it until I see it!"

Then we are like Kathy and the other disciples: we help other people to believe. We show them the signs.

JAMIE'S WAY

We all wish we could have a day like Thomas, when we get it absolutely clear and straight—when we see for our own eyes that it's true, that Jesus rose from the dead. Instead we have to go by the signs. But Jesus' promise is that one day we will all get to see him. It will be clear as day. We will all become apostles—people who have seen the risen Lord.

In the meantime, we'll be blessed—just for believing, for hanging on, for asking those questions, until we *really* see.

THINGS TO THINK ABOUT

How do you know when your parents are home? What kind of signs do they leave around?

Can you think of some signs Jesus gives us that he is really risen from the dead?

Would you like to see Jesus, yourself? What do you think that would be like?

PRAYING TOGETHER

"Lord Jesus Christ, your disciples were amazed to hear that you had risen from the dead. Some of them believed that it was true before they even saw you. Help us to believe until we can really see that you are risen; let us see with our own eyes just as soon as we're ready. Amen."

THE BLUE WATCHBAND GIRLS

"The kingdom of heaven may be compared to a king who gave a wedding banquet for his son. He sent his slaves to call those who had been invited to the wedding banquet, but they would not come. Again he sent other slaves, saying, 'Tell those who have been invited: Look, I have prepared my dinner, my oxen and my fat calves have been slaughtered, and everything is ready; come to the wedding banquet.' But they made light of it and went away, one to his farm, another to his business, while the rest seized his slaves, mistreated them, and killed them.... Then he said to his slaves, 'The wedding is ready, but those invited were not worthy. Go therefore into the main streets, and invite everyone you find to the wedding banquet.' Those slaves went out into the streets and gathered all whom they found, both good and bad; so the wedding hall was filled with guests." Matthew 22:2-10

Genevieve Moreau was depressed. She came home, slung her books on the kitchen table, and sat down to sulk. Alicia Crannell was giving another party for the Blue Watchband Girls.

The Blue Watchband Girls weren't a club, exactly—they just all happened to wear the same watchband, navy blue with red embroidery. Some had strawberries, some had

THE BLUE WATCHBAND GIRLS

sailboats, and some had ducks. Alicia Crannell's father bought her a watchband with red lobsters on it and that was the neatest one.

Anybody could get a blue watchband with strawberries on it; that wasn't the point. The point was that the girls with blue watchbands just happened to be the most popular girls in Genevieve's school. They got the best grades. They wore the nicest clothes, they were good in sports, and they did everything together. They even got sick together. If Alicia Crannell had a cold, and had to stay inside during recess, they all had colds, and all had to stay inside!

Genevieve Moreau had a deep, inner longing to be one of the Blue Watchband Girls. And now they were having a party and of course Genevieve had not been invited. Genevieve Moreau was Genevieve MOROSE.

Mother said: "Well for heaven's sake, Genevieve, you can have your own party. We'll invite that cute little red-haired girl— what's her name, Bridget? And your best friend Megan, and Janine. I'm sure she never gets invited to these things, either."

Genevieve scowled.

"Megan's not my best friend. She never gave my bracelet back. And Bridget has buck teeth. And don't even mention Janine, she is so dumb! And besides, it could never be as neat as Alicia's party. Her grandmother tells fortunes and they're making chocolate chip cookies from scratch that are better than anything you ever tasted, and they're all sleeping over. And, oh yuk. It's disgusting. I never get to go!"

"Genny," her mother said, "drink your tea, dear." She was smiling but Genevieve knew it meant "End of conversation." She grabbed her books and went to her room to sulk some more.

Next day, the telephone rang and Genevieve Moreau had quite a surprise. It was Alicia Crannell's grandmother.

"Genevieve, dear, you remember me, don't you? Well, I was wondering if you could come to Alicia's party tonight. Yes, I know it's late, but so many of the other girls are busy, Lord knows doing what, and Alicia is in tears. But she'd love to see you, and little Bridget, and what's her name—Megan? And who is this Janine Alicia's always complaining about—might as well call her, too! The more, the merrier, I always say—and do ask your mother to buy chocolate chips. We're going to need a bushel!"

Genevieve grinned and hung up the phone. "Whoopie!" she yelled, and told her mother. Then she sat right down and called Megan and Bridget and Janine. They all went and had such a good time.

Saturday morning Genevieve told her mother all about the party. Alicia's mother gave them all pink headbands to wear, and they ate SO MUCH CHOCOLATE but there was still enough left for the cookies, and Alicia Crannell asked to sit with her, Genevieve, at choir practice on Monday.

Alicia and Genevieve came to be friends, and you know it's a funny thing—once they'd become friends, Genevieve forgot all about the blue watchbands and the Blue Watchband Girls. And she never really minded being invited at the last minute because, well, being friends was what she wanted.

Jesus said: "This is what the kingdom of heaven is like. A king gave a wedding feast for his son, but at the last minute, nobody came. So he sent out into the streets and let anybody he could find come, whether they were nice or not. And there was room for them all."

Or, to put it another way, being part of God's kingdom is like being invited to the greatest party the world has ever known—not because you're special, or smart, or pretty, or rich, but just because God wants you to come. God's kingdom is like a heavenly banquet, a ball with dancing, music, singing, glittering lights. It's by invitation only. But the good news is, absolutely everybody is invited. And it's such a terrific thing that when you're there, you don't care who else got in, or whether you were invited first or last. You just want to be there. It's a place where everyone is included, and everyone has a good time.

When my daughter Kirsten was just a toddler, she always wanted to be included.

Whenever her father and I sat down to dinner, she used to come over to my chair and say "Uppy!" It didn't matter that she had already had her dinner. She still said "Uppy!" which was her version of "Up, please!" If I gave her a bottle, she threw it down; if I gave her a bite of my supper, she pulled on my leg. Uppy! Uppy, uppy, uppy, uppy!

She wanted to be included. So we taught her to use a spoon and fork. And soon enough the day came along when she could pull up a chair for herself. She was right, you know. She belonged at the table with us and the sooner we included her, the sooner she could grow into her full stature at that table.

That's how it is with God's kingdom. Once you're included, you grow. You start acting like you're somebody because God loves you—and bit by bit you're able to be a little kinder, a little stronger, more faithful and more loving.

That's the other part of the parable. Jesus said, "Once you've come to the wedding feast, you'd better dress for the occasion." When we accept the invitation to God's

JAMIE'S WAY

kingdom, we rise to the occasion, we act the part, we *become* the people God is calling us to be. When we accept the invitation, He gives us a place at His table, a chance to grow. Best of all, like Alicia in the story, He makes us His friends.

And for that delight we give Him thanks.

THINGS TO THINK ABOUT

Have you ever felt left out? What was that like? Was there anything you could do about it?

Can you imagine a school or a party where nobody has to feel left out? What would that be like?

Do you think heaven is a place where nobody feels left out? Is there anything we can do to make earth more like that now?

What sort of people is God looking for in His kingdom, do you think? Can you picture yourself as one of those people?

PRAYING TOGETHER

"Thank you, God, for inviting us to be part of your great kingdom. Help us to know what a special thing that is, and to say yes whenever you invite us. Make us the kind of people you would like around your table. Amen."

*L*OST AND FOUND

"I am the good shepherd. The good shepherd lays down his life for the sheep. The hired hand, who is not the shepherd and does not own the sheep, sees the wolf coming and leaves the sheep and runs away—and the wolf snatches them and scatters them. The hired hand runs away because a hired hand does not care for the sheep. I am the good shepherd. I know my own and my own know me, just as the Father knows me and I know the Father. And I lay down my life for the sheep."   John 10:11-15

When Mr. Atkins told his sixth grade class that they would be going to the Bronx Zoo, Billy Newcomb was thrilled. He loved the Bronx Zoo. He must have been there a hundred times with his mom and dad—well, maybe fifty times. Well, let's just say he'd been there. Four times. He had been to the Bronx Zoo four times, and he loved it.

He loved the monkey houses and he loved the open fields where the deer grazed. He loved the little round buildings, called kiosks, where his mother bought him cotton candy and hot dogs. Most of all he loved the great cats, and he memorized their names:

LOST AND FOUND

snow leopard, bobcat, jaguar, ocelot, lion, panther.

He couldn't wait to show his friends his favorite parts of the zoo. He felt that no one in his class could possibly be as familiar with the Bronx Zoo as he was—maybe not even Mr. Atkins, their teacher.

The day of the trip Billy was the first kid off the bus, after Mr. Atkins and Mrs. Peabody, the parent chaperone. They were supposed to have another parent along, Esthy Roberts' mother, but she had the flu and had to cancel at the last minute. So Mr. Atkins took Billy aside along with some of the other kids who had been to the zoo before and put them into a little group.

"I'm going to give you a map of the zoo. Billy, have you got a watch? Good. Now at exactly two o'clock—and I mean exactly, not a minute or two after—at exactly two o'clock, I want you to meet me right over there." He lifted his arm and pointed across the walkway to the main refreshment stand—a round, red-roofed building surrounded by picnic tables. "I'll see you there at two o'clock."

JAMIE'S WAY

"Oh, and there's one other thing," said Mr. Atkins as he handed out the maps. "It looks a bit like rain. If it should start to rain—even a little bit—come to the refreshment stand right away. We'll want to get everyone to the bus as quickly as possible so we can leave. Remember, don't talk to strangers, and meet us here at two o'clock."

And they were off. Mr. Atkins turned to another group of kids and headed off toward the elephants. Mrs. Peabody's group had already headed toward the monkeys. "All right, guys, let's hit the cats!" cried Billy, and that's just what they did. The six kids in the group headed for the cats. Then they went over to the elephants, then the bird house, then the polar bears. They were in a section that was just like the woods, looking for a koala bear that was supposed to be in the trees near them, when it started to rain.

"Hey, it's raining! Let's go back to the parking lot," said Billy.

"No, Billy, Mr. Atkins said to go to the refreshment stand!" said Judy Humphreys.

"Yeah, but the parking lot is closer. See on the map? That way we can get onto the bus. We'll surprise them!"

"No way, Billy, I'm going back to the refreshment stand," said Judy. "Me, too," said Sally, and Robert, and Jeffrey. That left Billy and Mark.

"C'mon, Mark, we'll show 'em," Billy said.

"Naw, I'm going with the others," said Mark. "See ya, Billy. Good luck."

Billy couldn't believe his ears. These were his friends. Why didn't they trust him? He knew he could find the parking lot, and it would be a lot faster. He'd show them.

He started running, his map in his hand. He turned left at the elephants and went down the hill. This had to be right; he could hear cars in the distance. But it was farther than he thought. It was really starting to rain now. He could hear the cars but was starting to wonder whether he was headed toward them or not. He stopped and opened his map to look, but it was hard to read in the rain. It looked like the parking lot was right near the elephants, but—ah, there it was. He turned again and ran, all the way to the parking lot. But when he got there, he stopped short. The lot was full of cars, but there were no school buses. Not a single one. "Something must be wrong," he thought. And then he panicked. Maybe they had left without him!

A car pulled up beside him and a man opened the door. "Hey, young man, you look like you're getting wet! Why don't you climb in the car here until your parents come? I'll wait with you," he offered.

Billy was about to open the back door of the car and get in when he thought better of it. This would not go over well at home. Even if the guy meant no harm, his parents would be really mad if they thought he'd gotten into a stranger's car.

"That's all right, man, really," he said, backing off. "Uh, thanks just the same." Billy's heart lurched in his chest. Was the man getting out of the car? He didn't take time to look. He ran, back towards the elephant fields, and up the path. He would have to go back to the refreshment stand and wait. Maybe he could find a phone and call home. Maybe somebody would be waiting for him there. He hoped so.

And then he heard a voice. "Billy!" it seemed to say. Could it be? He stopped and listened. It sounded far away. Maybe he was just hearing things. He was almost in tears. He hated being lost! "Billy, Billy Newcomb!" That time he heard it for sure. He couldn't be making that up!

"Billy!" He heard running feet. He turned around. It was Mr. Atkins, running with an umbrella. "Billy, where were you? We've been looking all over! Come on, the bus is waiting."

Thank God for Mr. Atkins, Billy thought. In a minute he knew Mr. Atkins would probably be scolding him for not following directions. But he didn't care. He was so grateful to be walking with somebody he knew. He touched Mr. Atkins' arm. "Boy, am I glad to see you!" he said. "I really got wet."

Mr. Atkins stopped. He looked at Billy for a minute. "Are you sure you're all right?"

"Sure, I'm all right—now. I'm all right now." He walked a few more feet. "Guess I went to the wrong parking lot."

JAMIE'S WAY

"Yeah," said Mr. Atkins.

"Aren't you going to yell at me?"

"Naw. I figure the kids are going to give you a pretty rough time anyway. They're all waiting in the bus. But next time, stick to the plan, all right?"

"All right," said Billy. "All right."

Nobody knows, really, if the stranger in the car meant Billy any harm. Some strangers do, you know. Just as in Jesus' time, there were lots of strangers trying to get Jesus' followers to do what they wanted instead of following Jesus.

Jesus told his followers not to worry. He knew all his followers by name, and they would always recognize his voice; even when they were lost, or out doing foolish things he'd told them not to do. That's Jesus' promise. Even when life gets scary, if we listen we can hear his voice. He can find us and take us home.

THINGS TO THINK ABOUT

Have you ever been lost? Where were you, and what was it like? How did you finally find your way?

Did anyone try to help you? Was it a stranger? Did you trust the stranger, or not? How did you decide whether to trust the stranger?

How can we tell the difference between someone who really cares for us, and someone who might cause us harm?

Why do you think Jesus compared himself to a shepherd? Was the teacher in the story a good shepherd?

What is it like, to hear Jesus' voice? Do we hear it with our ears? How can we know it's really Jesus?

PRAYING TOGETHER

"Lord Jesus Christ, you are our good shepherd. Help us to know your voice when we hear it so that we can follow you, and not be afraid. Keep us safe whenever we are lost! Amen."

A PERFECT GIFT

But when the goodness and loving kindness of God our Savior appeared, he saved us, not because of any works of righteousness that we had done, but according to his mercy through the water of rebirth and renewal by the Holy Spirit. This Spirit he poured out on us richly through Jesus Christ our Savior, so that, having been justified by his grace, we might become heirs according to the hope of eternal life. Titus 3:4-7

This Christmas Joey Blanchard had everything planned. In the way of presents, that is. He had worked on this list very carefully; he wrote down everything he wanted, and then picked out the things he wanted most and started a little campaign. Basically he wanted Muscle Men of the Universe, but he knew he wouldn't get much of it from his parents because they didn't approve of it—they said it was just a fad. They would think they were being terrific if they gave him the smallest set. He knew he would get plenty for Christmas—clothes, books, puzzles, things his parents thought he should have, and things his friends gave

A PERFECT GIFT

him. The question was whether he would get what he wanted, which was a lot of Muscle Men of the Universe stuff. Actually, not just a lot of it. All of it. He wanted all of it.

So Joey planned a campaign. He picked out a few friends and relatives, estimated what they were likely to spend, and made a list of the Muscle Men parts he wanted. Then he dropped hints— BIG hints—about each part to the person most likely to buy it for him. When he went to the movies with Tommy Jenkins, he said, just loud enough for Mrs. Jenkins to hear, "Gee, I sure wish I had the BX49 space shuttle attachment for my Muscle Men of the Universe set!" When he went to Toy Park with his cousin Adam, who was in college already and helping him to pick out a present for his baby sister, Joey took him to the space toys section and said, "WOW! An anti-matter neutralizer for Muscle Men of the Universe! And it's only thirteen dollars!"

But the king-pin in his plan was his Aunt Marie in Maine. Aunt Marie could always be counted on. She liked to buy toys, she didn't mind spending money, and she doted on Joey. Besides, she called on the phone every Thanksgiving Day just to ask what everybody wanted for Christmas that year.

This year Joey was ready for her.

"Get a pencil, Aunt Marie," he said. "I want the Muscle Men of the Universe advanced interstellar transport system. It has three extra characters in it and a shuttle craft. If you want, you can call this store in New York and have them send it to me—"

But before he could give the address of the store, his mother took the phone away from him, frowning.

"Mu-uh-ther!" Joey protested.

"Joey, it's fine to make gift suggestions for people, but giving the address of the store is going a little too far."

He shrugged. "I was only trying to help."

That was the last conversation he'd had with Aunt Marie since Thanksgiving. He started to worry. The days passed and nothing arrived in the mail. It wasn't until Christmas Eve Day, just as his family was going out the door to the Candlelight Service at church, that a battered cardboard box

A PERFECT GIFT

postmarked from Maine and covered in tape arrived. Joey begged his mother to unpack the box so that he could at least see the shape and size of his present, but she refused. He would just have to wait. All during church he fumed and fidgeted. How could he be sure he'd gotten what he wanted?

Early in the morning Joey rushed to the Christmas tree to find his gifts. He got the space shuttle attachment, and the anti-matter neutralizer. He got the books, puzzles, and records he expected. Joey saved Aunt Marie's present for last. He was sure it was the big red package in the back, the one with the shiny paper...but no, that was for his sister.

"Hey Mom, where's the package from Aunt Marie?" he asked. She handed him a slim package no bigger than his hand. It had a note on it that read:

"Dear Joey, I know you wanted something else this Christmas, but your Uncle Warren wanted you to have this as soon as you were old enough. I think you're old enough now. Love, Aunt Marie."

His heart sank. The package was too small to be the transport system, or any of the Muscle Men things. Knowing Uncle Warren, it could be anything—Uncle Warren was a little strange. Very careful about everything, especially his tools.

With a sigh Joey pulled the paper back and saw, to his surprise, an old blue box that he somehow remembered. He opened it and found his uncle's pocket knife.

He whistled, long and low. Uncle Warren's pocket knife! Joey remembered begging to use it, but he hadn't even been allowed to touch it. He pried open the blades, and checked to see if the bottle opener was still there on the other side. It was. So was the ivory toothpick.

Joey didn't know what to make of the knife. It wasn't that he didn't want it, because he'd always wanted it and never dreamed he'd get it. But it wasn't new. And it wasn't anything you could play with, really. Why did Aunt Marie think he was old enough? He didn't feel old enough. And he missed Uncle Warren, but....It was still on his mind that he wanted to get the rest of

A PERFECT GIFT

the Muscle Men set. Maybe Robby Barker next door got the interstellar set. Maybe he could trade the knife, or sell it. He heard himself gasp just thinking about it. He couldn't do that! He was going to have to keep the knife, and go without the transport system.

"Well, Joey," his dad said, "what do you think of that knife?"

"It's real nice, Dad."

"You're awfully quiet about it."

"It's just that I—you know—it's kind of a surprise. It's old. Like Uncle Warren."

Later, though, when he was in his room, he took the knife out again. Just holding it in his hands, he could see Uncle Warren, and it was hard to be reminded just how much he missed him. He could almost smell the tobacco in his uncle's pipe, watch him take out the smallest blade of the knife and tamp the tobacco down, then close the knife against his leg. Joey tried that, opening the knife, then closing it against his leg. He watched himself open it again, in the mirror this time, and wondered if he was old enough to smoke a pipe yet. Probably not.

It was funny about the knife. Aunt Marie said he was old enough to get it, but he didn't feel old enough. Now that he had it, though, he was feeling a little older already. Maybe he had gotten taller? He put the navy blue box back on his dresser as he'd seen his uncle do so many times, so he'd be sure to put the penknife back in the box that night. For now he had things to do, like a space shuttle to assemble. Maybe that knife was the gift he wanted after all.

When Jesus came to the people of Israel, he wasn't exactly the king they were looking for. In fact, he came to them in the form of a child. Not a mighty warrior, or a fierce ruler, but a baby who grew up to be a healer and teacher. He was a poor man, born in a poor place. It was different than they might have expected.

And they probably didn't deserve Jesus, either, good as he was; they didn't appreciate what they had. Maybe they weren't quite ready. But God sent Jesus anyway, loving them the way Aunt Marie loved Joey. Not because he'd done anything special but because they were family, because she loved

A PERFECT GIFT

him, because his Uncle Warren had loved him.

Just getting the knife helped Joey grow. By the end of the day he was happy to have it. That's the way it is with God's gift to us—His great gift, the Christ child. We may not be ready to receive Jesus, but little by little we grow into it.

You know, I bet that Joey still had that knife ten years later, maybe even twenty years later. Maybe he gave it to his own nephew! The best gifts are like that—gifts for keeps. And this gift, this Christmas gift, is ours for keeps as well. God's own son, the Christ.

THINGS TO THINK ABOUT

What's the best Christmas gift you've ever gotten? Did you ask for it ahead of time? What was it like to receive it?

Why do you think his Aunt Marie gave him the knife instead of the gift he wanted?

Do you think Joey expected that he would have the knife someday, or was it a complete surprise? How did he feel about the knife when he got it? Have you ever felt that way about a gift?

Was Joey's Aunt Marie right to send him the knife? Do you think he deserved it? Was he old enough to use it properly?

What kinds of gifts does God give to people? Is there a gift you wish God would give you?

PRAYING TOGETHER

Close your eyes and think for just a minute about the gift you would like from God.

"Lord God, thank you for giving the world so many gifts. Help us to receive the gifts you give us, and to use them well, even when they're not what we expect. Amen."

"AND YOU'LL WEAR DIAMONDS"

In those days Jesus came from Nazareth of Galilee and was baptized by John in the Jordan. And just as he was coming up out of the water, he saw the heavens torn apart and the Spirit descending like a dove upon him. And a voice came from heaven, "You are my Son, the Beloved; with you I am well pleased."

And the Spirit immediately drove him out into the wilderness. He was in the wilderness forty days, tempted by Satan; and he was with the wild beasts; and the angels waited on him.   Mark 1:9-13

Jonathan Healy was bored. He was bored in church. They had only gotten as far as the first lesson for the day, and already he had looked at every page in his prayerbook and looked up all his favorite hymns in the hymnal. When he started swaying and humming, his mother took the hymnal away and shushed him. Jonathan slid down in the pew and tucked his toes up under the hymnal rack ahead, and pushed his heels where the small of Mrs. Johnson's back would be in the next pew. His mother shoved his legs down and told him to sit up straight.

"Why don't you sit up and listen?!" she hissed. Jonathan looked at her sideways and shrugged his shoulders. Not much to listen to, as far as he could tell. Dr. Rockleberry came down the aisle, though, close to them, and read from a big red leather book. At least that was worth watching, because Allison Haymeyer, the blonde fifth grader, was holding her torch up crooked in the procession. Jonathan liked that part; he liked wondering if she was going to catch her hair on fire.

Dr. Rockleberry was reading something about Jesus being baptized in the Jordan River. Boy, he had all the fun, Jonathan thought. He didn't have to put on a tie and sit in a wooden pew next to his mother. He got to go out to the Jordan River, which wasn't even in America, for goshsakes, and get dunked. And then, Dr. Rockleberry said, he got to spend forty whole days out in the desert with monsters and ghosts and angels and things. Forty days with no school, no homework, no spinach to eat or eggplant or school lunch....Jesus had all the fun.

"And you'll wear diamonds"

Allison Haymeyer turned and walked away with Dr. Rockleberry following her. Jonathan sank down in his pew again, quietly snuck his feet back up to the next pew, and started thinking. "I wonder," he thought, "I wonder what it really would be like, getting baptized in the Jordan River?"

And he stared at his shoelaces and started to play his swimming pool game. This is the swimming pool game. You pretend you're going underwater, holding your breath, and bouncing your feet on the bottom of the pool. Every time you come up out of the water, you come up somewhere different. Like, the first time, you imagine coming up out of the pool and the sky is bright and blue and sunny, and then you go back down into the water. The next time you come up it's dark, and you're in a lake instead of a pool, and you can see the moon, and the next time you go under water and come up, you're in the ocean, jumping out with the dolphins, or maybe you *are* a dolphin, or even a whale.

Jonathan played the swimming pool game whenever he had to sit through a long speech, or bus ride, or when his teacher was yelling at him. So he settled down and played it in church, because the sermon was starting. Once, he bobbed down and came up in the sunshine. Once more, he bobbed down and came up in the lake. A third time he came up and—oh, boy, this was different! He was standing waist deep in some warm water, and before he even opened his eyes he noticed a great big hand was on the back of his neck. And there were voices all around him. Grown-ups, kids, women—their voices all sounded muffled, like voices at the beach. He opened his eyes and thought, "Wow, this must be the River Jordan!" Sure enough, there was a man with a beard holding on to him, and he lifted Jonathan way out of the water and put him back on shore, patted him roughly on the back, and said, "Go, Jonathan! Now! Go! Go on, get out of here."

And Jonathan took off running—he didn't know where—he just took off running, up the banks of the river toward a dirt road, and along the road toward a clump of trees, and up a hill, and over, into a flat and dry

"And you'll wear diamonds"

plain full of rocks. Finally he slowed up, because the sun was going down and he still didn't know where he was going. As it got darker, he shivered. He wasn't even dry yet. Around him, along the road, there were clumps of bushes and rocks. The darker it got, the further he walked, the more they looked like sleeping animals—elephants, some of them—tigers—one even had a long neck like a giraffe slung low, and it seemed to lift its head and look at him. He blinked his eyes and shuddered. Where was he? He heard an owl laughing and hooting, and the strangest, saddest dove, and he wondered where they all could be. He imagined he heard the hissing of a snake.

Jonathan felt around in his pockets for something to eat. Sure enough, there was something there, an old wet piece of French bread. Ugh! he thought. I'll try that later. He was feeling that piece of French bread in his pocket when, at the top of the next rise, he saw a wooden shack, a fruit stand like the ones they have in the country. There was a strange man standing inside it, a man who looked just like the old count on

Sesame Street but much more—what was the word Mom liked to use?—sinister. Yes, that was it. He was sinister. There was a strange light in the booth and a creepy light around his face. But he was somehow appealing; he smiled a lot. He was tossing a coin up and down. He said "Welcome, Jonathan. I've been waiting for you."

Jonathan said, "Who are you?"

"Don't you want to hear your fortune?"

"Wait a minute. Who are you? What is this, some kind of carnival?"

"No, my boy. All you have to do is listen to me. We'll just flip this coin and see what will be happening to you. Maybe you'll have to stay at school—maybe you won't! You said you were just baptized, eh? Going to be good, eh? Maybe you will"—he flipped the coin—"and maybe you won't. You want to know if your sick little doggie will get better? Maybe he will"—flip!—"and maybe he won't. Who knows, Jonathan? There's no guarantee, is there? Why don't you just stay here with me and have some of this nice, shiny apple?"

"And you'll wear diamonds"

Jonathan could barely hear what the man was saying. Something about him made him want to stay, but he didn't really want to. Then he took a breath and noticed something; the whole place smelled bad. Really bad. "Oh, my God," he thought, "What's that? That's terrible. That's like that old fish we found dead on the beach last summer. That smells like death. That's what it is." His eyes grew wide. "And that's the devil! But I don't even believe in the devil, do I?" A chill ran from the base of his spine to the top of his head.

"Yikes!" he yelled. And turned. And ran. Back down the road. And his feet—this was weird—his feet leapt up higher than they ever had before, and his lungs filled with air as though they were balloons, and his knees held up, and he didn't stumble, he didn't trip on his shoelaces, he just ran and ran, his legs stretching out and as he ran the light came up again and he found that brown river and he went splashing into it and laughing and held his breath and plunged in and came up and....

Well, Jonathan was supposed to be back in church but he wasn't. He wasn't sure where he was. Only he knew that he was all right, he was more than all right. He was absolutely blessed.

And his life, all the years ahead of him, stretched beyond him like a river. His life and his breath and the sky were all around him like a river, and he knew he must really be in church, because for the first time in his life he was talking to God and God was talking to him. But not with words. His heart was talking to God and God was talking back, way inside him. It was like his insides talking to his insides and he couldn't even translate.

There weren't any words to it, it was more like a song. A song, yes, and his mouth was full of it and any minute now he was going to blurt it out. And just when he thought it would burst out of his mouth he felt a pressure on his arm, his mother shaking him. He opened his eyes just in time to see the minister up front raising the great silver cup. Jonathan got up out of his seat, he stood up in church, and Dr. Rockle-

"AND YOU'LL WEAR DIAMONDS"

berry—he could have sworn it—Dr. Rockleberry caught his eye and winked.

Jonathan went up for communion, and that's when he knew what it was—what God had said. He started to laugh because it was something Gramps was always saying to Jonathan's mom when she was confused, or tired, or discouraged, or when she was wondering what would happen next. "Stick with me, kid, and you'll wear diamonds." That was the message. "Stick with me, and you'll wear diamonds."

In those days Jesus came from Nazareth of Galilee and was baptized by John in the Jordan. And just as he was coming up out of the water, he saw the heavens torn apart and the Spirit descending like a dove on him. And a voice came from heaven, "You are my Son, the Beloved; with you I am well pleased." The Spirit immediately drove him out into the wilderness. He was in the wilderness forty days, tempted by Satan; and he was with the wild beasts; and the angels waited on him.

THINGS TO THINK ABOUT

Have you ever been bored in church? What do you do to pass the time when you're bored?

Have you ever imagined what it would be like to meet the devil? Is that who Jonathan met out there by the fruit stand?

Was Jonathan's daydream like Jesus' baptism? Do you think that's what it was like for Jesus to be tempted in the wilderness?

PRAYING TOGETHER

Close your eyes for a minute and imagine that you are with Jesus in the wilderness. Who is out there with you? What do they look like?

"Lord Jesus, we're glad that you were baptized and went into the wilderness. We're glad you didn't stay in the wilderness too long. Thank you for showing us the way. Amen."

IT'S THE PITS!

"For to all those who have, more will be given, and they will have an abundance; but from those who have nothing, even what they have will be taken away." Matthew 25:29

Peter Caulfield sat on his big sister Julie's bed and helped her to pack for camp. Rather he was watching her pack for camp—sorting out which things she would need for her summer job as a camp counselor and which things she would leave home. So many decisions! Which shorts, which sweatshirts, which stuffed animals, which bracelets?

Actually, he wasn't that interested in the clothes and stuff. Peter was interested in her plants. Julie had won a prize in a science fair with her Boston fern, and she was so good with plants that some of their mother's friends asked her for advice when theirs got brown, or droopy, or whatever plants did when they were sick. Peter hoped she would leave some of her plants with him. Especially the prize-winning Boston fern. That was his favorite.

But Julie had already decided to leave the Boston fern with her friend Natalie to look after, and her great spider plant and coleus to somebody named Susie. But next to the coleus on her window sill was this funny, egg-shaped brown thing that wasn't even a plant. It was wrinkly, almost hairy.

"Yuk, Julie," he said. "This is u-u-ugly. What are you going to do with this, play ball with it?"

"No, stupid," she said. "That's an avocado pit. Mom used an avocado in the salad last week and I saved the pit to start an avocado tree. Only the pit isn't ready. You see, it's going to dry up and crack a little bit. Then you just plop it over a glass of water and bingo! you've got a little tree. In fact, why don't you take care of it? It's all yours."

Peter tried hard to conceal his disappointment. He wanted something more important than a dumb old avocado pit. He didn't see how it could ever turn into a tree.

Anyway, Julie left for camp, and just as she had said, the pit dried out and the outer skin cracked. Peter propped the pit up over a glass of water, using toothpicks to hold it

*I*T'S THE PITS!

in place. It was so easy it was stupid. The seed opened, and thread-like roots popped out of the bottom, and a slim green stem pushed its way out the top. That was that. Peter put the glass on the window sill in Julie's room and left it.

Late in July Julie got a weekend off and came home for a few days. First thing, she went round to check on her plants. The Boston fern was doing so well at Natalie's that their Mom made Julie write a thank-you note, and Susie's spider plant had had given birth to a baby spider plant big enough for its own pot already. But it wasn't until the second day that Julie remembered to ask Peter about the avocado pit—and by this time he had forgotten all about it.

"Hey, Peter—what happened to the avocado pit I left you? Where's my tree?"

"Didn't you see it? It's on your window sill."

Julie went to her room, and saw the seed, and stormed back out, carrying it in her hand. The water around it was all brown, the glass was full of roots, and the spindly stem leaned downward from the top like a dog drooping its head. A few drops of murky water clung to the bottom of the glass.

"Peter!" she yelled. "How could you be so dumb! You left it in the sun all that time. You obviously didn't water it. It should have been planted in dirt by now, and have leaves and everything! You can't leave a plant like that! Oh Peter, can't I trust you with anything? I'm going to pot this up and give it to Natalie. Maybe she can do something with it. Golly, I thought this would be a whole tree by now. I wish you would pay more attention."

Peter flushed. "Gee, Julie, I didn't know you had to put it in dirt. And besides, that's not a tree, it's just a little stick! And when you gave it to me it was just an ugly old seed!"

"Peter, you are truly average and dumb. You should use your imagination."

Peter went back to his own room because he was close to tears. Of course he was disappointed that he didn't have a tree to show for Julie. But more than that, he was upset because she was so mad. It was terrible to have her angry with him, especially when

*I*T'S THE PITS!

she was just home for a few days from camp. He was mad, too, but still he promised himself next time Julie gave him anything he would take good care of it. It wasn't worth it, having her mad at him like that.

Jesus told a story about a wealthy man who took a long trip. Before he left, this man divided his money among three servants and asked them to look after it for him. He gave five talents of money to his first servant; two to another, and to the last servant he gave only one. The first two servants invested their money in business projects and doubled what he had given them. The third fellow hid the money so he wouldn't lose a penny. When the owner came back, he was thrilled with the first two servants and rewarded them with even more money, but he was very angry with the third servant. That servant was in trouble—he had not earned any money with his talent and his master was furious. It probably made him very sad.

Have you got a talent? I don't mean tap-dancing, or making great brownies, or that kind of stuff. I mean a special part of the world to look after. God's world is His treasure and He assigns little parts of it for each of us to look after, just the way Julie divided up her plants. I wonder what part He's assigning to you.

Are you the only kid in the class who doesn't laugh when stammering Joe gets all tongue-tied? Are you somebody's best friend? Are you somebody's *only* friend? Do you have a special way with your baby brother? Do you have a secret talent? Maybe nobody knows about it—maybe you don't even know yet!

So you think your talent is the pits, just an avocado pit. Maybe you think nothing can come of it. God knows that with a little bit of effort, and some imagination, a pit could turn into a tree. A little talent can go a long way. That's why Jesus tells us we've got to look sharp, and use what we have—no matter how little or insignificant we think it is.

You know that one talent the last servant had? Do you know how much money it really was? Well, if we take the standards of

It's the Pits!

living today, and think how much that talent would have bought, it comes to about two thousand dollars. That was the least of the master's gifts. Just imagine what your talent from God must be worth! Pay attention. Use your imagination. Make it grow.

THINGS TO THINK ABOUT

What is a talent, really? How do you know when you have one?

Why do think God gives different talents to different people? Is it fair?

What can we do when we're disappointed in our abilities—our gifts?

What talents do you have? Why do you think God gave them to you? Do you think there might be something special He would like you to do? (You don't have to tell; just think about it.)

PRAYING TOGETHER

Close your eyes and imagine yourself doing something you like to do—something that really interests you, something that does some good. It doesn't have to be something you do well. Now imagine God watching you, and smiling.

"Thank you, God, for giving us different abilities and interests. Help us to use every little gift you give us, and not to be discouraged when the gift looks small. Help us to make your gifts grow. Amen."

ALMOST PERSUADED

Then the devil took him to Jerusalem, and placed him on the pinnacle of the temple, saying to him, "If you are the Son of God, throw yourself down from here, for it is written,
> *'he will command his angels*
> *concerning you,*
> *to protect you,'*
> *and*
> *'On their hands they will bear*
> *you up,*
> *so that you will not dash your*
> *foot against a stone.'"*

Jesus answered him, "It is said, 'Do not put the Lord your God to the test.'" When the devil had finished every test, he departed from him until an opportune time. Luke 4:9-13

Joey Henderson was not the kind of guy who cheats in school, at least not so far. He'd gotten all the way to the seventh grade without doing it. For one thing, Joey Henderson was pretty smart. And he took school seriously, so he didn't need to borrow anybody's homework the way some guys did. Besides, he didn't believe in cheating. He thought it was wrong.

It came as a surprise, then, the day he almost did cheat.

At St. Christopher's, where he went to Sunday School, they had just been studying about temptation. They'd read the story about Jesus' temptation, and Joey heard how Jesus had been taken out into the wilderness, and how Satan had shown him all the nations of the world and said: "All this and more is yours if you will follow me." And how he tried to get Jesus to turn the stones to bread and even throw himself off buildings so that the angels would pick him up. Joey liked the story—and even more than that, he liked making temptations for himself.

LIKE—temptation is when you're offered a job as an enemy spy for a lot of money—or when you're a prisoner of war and they torture you and they put the screws to your hands and try to get top secret information out of you—or when the big guys from the high school come down with a lot of drugs and try to get you to use them. To get you to be, you know, like them.

He spent his time in class daydreaming about being out in the wilderness himself. Joey liked jungle temptations better, so he'd dream he was out in the jungle, being tempted. He liked to daydream about Darth Vader, the big ugly robot in *Star Wars,* and Darth Vader would try to get him to agree to sign his life over to the forces of evil, in return for which Joey would receive a Porsche, a Maserati, and a great ranch in the West from which he would control a vast underground empire. Ah, temptation! "All this is yours," Darth Vader might say, "if you will follow me, and serve the forces of evil." So Joey Henderson thought he understood temptation pretty well.

Until the day it happened to him.

He was taking a test in his music appreciation class. Joey thought it was a stupid test, first of all, because you had to memorize a lot of names and dates for it. He didn't like to memorize names and dates. Also, you have to understand that Joey was a student with Serious Ambitions, and he knew that his grades in music appreciation were not taken as seriously as his grades in, say, social studies, science, or English. He figured as long as he could keep a good easy "B" in music appreciation, that was enough. After all, it was an elective. Besides, there was a lot of music in his family, people who played instruments and things, and he sang in the choir at church. Joey figured he knew a lot about music, at least compared to other kids, so he shouldn't have to study for a music test.

So Joey was surprised and a little humiliated to find out that this test was a good deal harder than he'd expected. In fact, he was doing pretty badly. He was supposed to write down the year that Mozart was born, and he couldn't remember when Mozart lived at all. To tell you the truth, he'd never learned when Mozart lived, or even where. There was no point in trying to remember, as if it might come back to him. He just didn't know.

He was sitting chewing on his pencil and wondering what to do about the fact that he was probably going to fail this test, when Howie Jenkins, who was sitting beside him, whispered to him.

"Joey!"

Howie was not the most popular kid in the school—he was fat, his grades were terrible, and he didn't have very many friends.

"Joey!"

To his horror, Joey saw that Howie had taken his test sheet and shifted it to the side of the desk so that Joey could see every answer on the page.

"Joey! Seventeen!"

He was trying to tell Joey some of the answers to the test. Joey shot a glance at the paper. Howie must really have studied for this test. There was something written beside every number on his paper; he had an answer for everything! Joey couldn't figure this out, because Howie wasn't that smart. And then he remembered what Howie's parents did. They were both involved with the opera. Joey bet that every single answer on that sheet was right.

"Joey! Come on!" hissed Howie, nudging Joey with his elbow.

Then he thought, well, Howie doesn't have any friends and it's really nice that he's trying to help me out. Joey started thinking about how maybe Howie wanted to be friends and that's why he was doing this, and Joey did feel sorry for Howie, and, well, maybe this was just Howie's way of trying to be friends. After all, who was he to refuse an offer of help from some poor kid who didn't have any friends? Maybe this was something that God was calling him to do, to help Howie out. Anyway, maybe he could just look at one or two answers, just enough so that he could pass. It wasn't an important test.

Howie looked at him and winked. Joey turned beet red and shook his head no. He felt horribly embarrassed. Howie shrugged, pulled his paper over to the other side of the desk. Now Howie's face was red, too.

Joey heaved a sigh of relief. His heart was pounding. His hand was shaking. Then he started to giggle. He looked at his paper. He decided he would say that Mozart was born in 700 B.C. If he was going to fail this test, he was at least going to fail it in style.

The bell rang and he turned in his paper. He was worried about the grade he was going to get on this test. And he knew that Mr. Peabody, the teacher, was going to scowl at him when he passed it back with a bad grade on it. Still, when he got to the door Joey thumped Howie on the back, hard, and practically yelled, "Howie, old buddy, how are things at the opera?"

He walked on to his next class, daydreaming. Here he was. He had survived temptation in music appreciation class. Nobody knew. He wasn't even going to get a good grade on the test. And it was weird, you know—temptation wasn't like Darth Vader at all. It was tiny, it was tricky. For a minute there, Joey even thought he'd be helping somebody else out if he cheated on that test. Temptation was subtle, and it came when he was least expecting it. It was something that wasn't even that important. It made him wonder—he'd almost given in to Howie Jenkins—what would he have done if it was really the Devil?

Joey smiled, got to his desk in his next class, and looked up Mozart's birthday: 1756. Oh, well. Only about 2400 years off.

And then he thought: If Jesus got through all of that, he must have been quite a guy.

THINGS TO THINK ABOUT

What was so tricky about Joey's temptation? Did you think that he would give in to it?

Would Joey and Howie have become friends if he had taken Howie's answers for the test?

Have you ever been tempted like that? Maybe you'd like to talk about it. (Maybe you'd rather not!) How did it turn out?

How was Jesus strong against temptation? Do you think the things the devil suggested to him were really tempting to him, the way Howie's help with the test would have been tempting to Joey? How did the devil know how to tempt him?

What do you think it means, that the devil went away from Jesus "until an opportune time?"

PRAYING TOGETHER

Close your eyes and think for a minute: is there something you've been tempted to do lately, something that might hurt someone else, or even hurt yourself? Imagine yourself about to do that thing. Now imagine that Jesus is with you as you think about it.

"Lord Jesus, we are glad that you were tempted. We are tempted lots of times, and it isn't always easy, not giving in. Help us to be strong; help us to remember to ask for your help when the going gets rough. Amen."

I WANT IT NOW!

When the Pharisees heard that he had silenced the Sadducees, they gathered together, and one of them, a lawyer, asked him a question to test him. "Teacher, which commandment in the law is the greatest?" He said to him, "'You shall love the Lord your God with all your heart, and with all your soul, and with all your mind.' This is the greatest and first commandment. And a second is like it: 'You shall love your neighbor as yourself.' On these two commandments hang all the law and the prophets." Matthew 22:34-40

It all started at McDonald's. Josie McHendricks had gone there after school alone on Thursday. Halloween was coming up, and she wanted to see what the special was. Usually they had some kind of kids' special, a Happy Meal, that you got with your hamburger, french fries, and soda. Josie had heard that the kids' special this week offered a plastic pumpkin with face paints inside it, and she wanted the face paints for her Halloween costume. Otherwise she was a little old for a Happy Meal—she hadn't had one since she was nine, and now she was twelve. But she thought it would be fun to get one today

I WANT IT NOW!

and see who else was hanging out after school.

There were plenty of kids there, all right, but none of them from her school. Even so, it was more crowded than she had ever seen it, probably because of the Halloween specials. Josie got in line—a long line, even for McDonald's—and looked up at the promotional posters behind the counter. Oh, good, she was right: the Happy Meal was a hamburger inside a plastic pumpkin. She saw somebody at a table near the door opening one, and pulling out the face paint. It was just what she wanted.

She stood in line for what seemed a very long time, thinking about what kind of soda she would order with the Happy Meal, counting her money to be sure she had enough. The boy in front of her seemed to be doing the same thing; she didn't think she'd ever seen him before, but he looked to be about her age.

When she finally got to the front of the line she asked for the Happy Meal, and waited, but the girl behind the counter just looked at her and said, "We're out." Just like that! Josie could hardly believe it. McDonald's was never out of stuff.

She looked to the front of the line next to her and saw that the kid at the next register had a pumpkin, and the boy who had been in front of her had gotten one, too. "Wait a minute," she said, "they got the Happy Meal! How come I can't have one?" But the girl just shook her head. "Last one," she said. "We're all out."

Josie was devastated. She stood there, pouting a little, not saying anything. She was thinking.

"Well," said the girl, "are you going to order or not?"

"Oh all right," Josie answered. "Just give me a diet coke—*large*."

The girl turned and stepped away from the counter and Josie looked around her at the crowd. What a bunch of scuzzy-looking kids, she thought. How crummy that they all get pumpkins and face paints and I don't. And I needed that face paint for my costume!

The girl returned to the counter and tapped Josie on the shoulder; "Miss," she

I WANT IT NOW!

said, "we're all out of diet coke! Would you like something else? We have orange, and we have regular coke, but we're all out of the diet."

Josie looked at her in disbelief. Out of diet coke? This was not to be believed. "No," she said, still surprised, "I don't want anything else." She left the counter still muttering to herself. "I don't want anything else. I want diet coke—I want the Happy Meal!" And much to her embarrassment, tears began to well up in her eyes.

Then she saw the boy who had been right in front of her. "Hey, I got a pumpkin," he said, waving a plastic pumpkin in the air. "You want it?"

"Yes! Yes, I do!" she said, brightening. This guy was going to give her his pumpkin!

"Well too bad, 'cause I want it too!" he shouted, and pulled the pumpkin back under his arm.

"Awwwww," he said as she pressed between the aisles toward the door to get out, "Look at that—she's all disappointed.

Awwwww." He was making fun of her! In front of all his friends!

Josie stepped outside to the shelter at the bus stop and leaned against its wall. "Of course I want the stupid pumpkin," she thought. "That's why I went in there in the first place." She kept hearing that boy's voice, though, in her head: I want it, too. I want it, too.

Well, he can keep his old pumpkin, she thought; if he wanted it the way I wanted it, he might as well keep it.

Josie rode the bus home, sulking. She went to her room, slung her books on the bed, and started to change her clothes. Just as she lifted her arms to take off her sweater she noticed, on the corner of her dresser, her silver charm bracelet.

She picked it up and started to put it on, pausing for a moment to look at the charms she liked best: the little silver Scotty dog, the tiny cup and saucer. She sat down on the bed and looked at the charms, one by one. Looking up, she noticed her little sister Adele at the door. Adele was biting her lip,

I WANT IT NOW!

watching her with the bracelet, as if she had something to say.

"Josie, Jennifer Perkins came to school with another bracelet today. When can I wear your bracelet, please? Pleeeeeease?"

"Wear this bracelet? You don't mean it," Josie said, giving her a hard stare. Adele was so irresponsible, always losing things. Already she could see the bracelet dragging through ketchup, getting caught in the bus door, or worse, falling off Adele's skinny little arm. She was just about to say, "No way, Jose! Forget it! Not now, not ever will you wear this bracelet. Don't even think about it!" She held up the bracelet to say all that, and then stopped.

She was rememembering that awful boy at McDonald's. She could just see him waving that pumpkin at her; she could hear him saying, "Awwww, she's disappointed!" And she could feel her face getting red again, just at the thought of him. Boy, she thought, is that what Adele feels like? Am I going to make Adele feel the way I felt at McDonald's?

It wasn't worth it. With a kind of sick feeling in her stomach, she changed her mind. "Hold out your hand," she said wearily, and dropped the bracelet into her little sister's hand. "Only don't get it wet, don't get it caught in any doors, and don't let it fall off your wrist! You got that?"

She looked up. Adele's face was pink with pleasure, and surprise. Her eyes were wide, her mouth agape. "Oh, goodeeee!" she started to squeal, and threw her arms around her Josie's neck. "I love you, Josie! I love you so much! You're the best sister in the whole wide world!"

"Huh!" thought Josie. "Best sister in the whole world! That's not bad!" She grinned, in spite of herself.

Once in Galilee Jesus met some people who had a question about being the best— about how people ought to live the best way. The way they put it, though, was to ask him a question about the Law. By "the Law" they meant the whole teaching about how somebody ought to live. Say you wanted to live a good life, a happy, healthy, full life—

how do you do it? What's the first step? Jesus didn't answer them with one law, he answered them with two.

Jesus said, "You shall love the Lord your God with all your heart, with all your soul, and all your mind," and "You shall love your neighbor as yourself."

The law about loving other people came second, but it would be a mistake to think it was less important. The two laws go together.

Then Jesus said "On these two commandments hang all the Law and the Prophets." That is—if you get these two down, you've basically got the whole thing. That's how to have a good life. Love God, and do for others what you'd like them to do for you.

Everybody doesn't want exactly what you want. In a matter of choice, you might like red, another person might like blue. You might like to be at the beach in the summer, another person might like to go to the mountains. People want different things at different times, but underneath they're surprisingly the same. Certainly we all *need* pretty much the same things. You might want a red sweater and another person a blue sweater, but you both want to feel warm and look good. You might want a room of your own; your sister might want a room of her own, too. Basically what you both want is a nice place to live.

The point is, you have a ready-made measuring stick of how kind you ought to be to other people. And that measuring stick is this: they just might want exactly what you want. If they did, how would you act? If the kid sitting next to you at school wanted exactly what you wanted, how would you treat that kid? If your younger sister or your younger brother wanted exactly what you want, how would you act?

A lot of the time it will turn out that they want something different. But the Christian way is to give your younger brother or sister, the other kid at school, and eventually the people you meet in the world the benefit of the doubt. You give them that much respect. It just might be possible that they want exactly what you want. A nice roof over their heads, a new sweater, some-

I WANT IT NOW!

thing good to eat, some friends, a hug, a good life, a kind life.

Jesus put that practical way of thinking about what other people might want and what we want right up there with something as lofty-sounding as loving the Lord your God with all your heart, with all your soul, and with all your mind. The two are linked. Maybe because the other person you love by being kind is also someone that God loves; when you show kindness to another, you're helping God care for that person. And helping God is, well, it's breath-taking.

Think about those things this week. Love the Lord your God with all your heart and all your soul and all your mind; and love your neighbor—your brother, your sister, the kids at school, the people you meet—the way you'd like to be loved yourself.

THINGS TO THINK ABOUT

Have you ever had something that somebody else wanted? What did you do? Were you able to find a way to share it? How did you feel about it?

Why do you think Jesus said you should love your neighbor as yourself? Can you think of an example of how you would do that?

PRAYING TOGETHER

"God give us the strength to follow your Law; teach us your ways, and show us pleasure in them. Amen."

*T*HE SKATING PARTY

Six days later, Jesus took with him Peter and James and John, and led them up a high mountain apart, by themselves. And he was transfigured before them, and his clothes became dazzling white, such as no one on earth could bleach them. And there appeared to them Elijah with Moses, who were talking with Jesus. Then Peter said to Jesus, "Rabbi, it is good for us to be here; let us make three dwellings, one for you, one for Moses, and one for Elijah." He did not know what to say, for they were terrified. Then a cloud overshadowed them, and from the cloud there came a voice, "This is my Son, the Beloved; listen to him!" Suddenly when they looked around, they saw no one with them any more, but only Jesus.

As they were coming down the mountain, he ordered them to tell no one about what they had seen....
Mark 9:2-9

Nobody thought he could skate. That's why the kids at St. John's Church were surprised when they heard the announcement: Mr. Adams, the sixth grade Sunday School teacher, was inviting all the kids to go on a winter hike, and ice skating, with him. Most of the kids didn't want to go, because they thought he couldn't skate.

Actually Mr. Adams was the hockey coach at the junior high school, but nobody had ever seen him out on the ice. He was always on the sidelines, yelling at his team. The team made out all right; he was a good coach and he seemed to know a lot about hockey. But since no one had ever seen Mr. Adams put on a pair of ice skates, they all thought he couldn't skate.

Besides, Mr. Adams had only been in their town about a year and a half; he had moved there from the big city. As far as the kids in Littleton, New York knew, city people didn't go ice skating.

So the kids were all pretty reluctant to go on this skating trip, and when the day came, a Saturday afternoon in the middle of February, almost no one turned up.

In fact, only three kids turned up. Amy Harrison—well, everybody figured she would go, because she was in Mr. Adams Sunday School class and had a crush on him. She thought he was wonderful. And the Barrie twins, Jessica and Peter—they went because it was a church activity, and their parents made them do everything at

THE SKATING PARTY

church. If the church opened its doors, the Barrie twins had to be there. "I went to church every Sunday growing up, and so can you," their father liked to say. So even if it was just ice skating—no Bible study or praying or anything— they had to go.

Not that they minded, really. They were sort of curious about Mr. Adams. Why did he want to go hiking in the middle of winter? And would he really skate, or just watch them? And why didn't he want to take them skating at the local ice rink where they usually went? What sort of person was he, anyway?

Mr. Adams kept saying there was a meadow out behind the high school that he wanted to explore, that there was a great pond back there for skating. Peter and Jessica had never seen the pond; Amy had never seen it, either. Even her dad had never seen the pond Mr. Adams was talking about, and he had grown up in Littleton. But it was worth a try.

"Be sure the ice is thick before you go out," Amy's father said to her as she got out of the car that day. "Let Mr. Adams test it first."

"Okay, Dad!" she answered. But what if he doesn't skate? she wondered to herself. What if he just lets us go out on the ice by ourselves? She shivered a bit, and it wasn't just the cold that made her do it.

She said hello to Mr. Adams, and Jessica, and Peter. They all gave one last wave to their parents as the cars pulled away. They pulled their mittens tight inside their sleeves, wrapped their scarves snug around their faces, slung their skates over their shoulders, and followed Mr. Adams in a little line, looking for the meadow and the pond in the meadow where they could skate.

It was cold. Amy felt her toes getting stiff even before they got to the high school, while Peter stopped and rewound his scarf twice. The sky was grey; a light, wet snow began to fall; the walk was long. Jessica Barrie was wondering why Mr. Adams would go to so much trouble just to find a new place to skate, when there was a perfectly good rink by the shopping mall out-

THE SKATING PARTY

side town. Out here they were going to get wet and cold.

She was grumbling to herself about that when they reached the top of a little hill, and she saw what Mr. Adams had been talking about. There was a pond, a lovely pond the shape of a long oval, surrounded by snow banks and dried weeds. There weren't even footprints in the snow around it. Nobody had been skating here at all.

"You kids put on your skates while I test the ice," Mr. Adams said, and sat down quickly to pull off his shoes. He reached into a shoulder bag and pulled out a very old pair of brown skates, skates not at all like the ones these kids had seen. They weren't at all slick like the hockey skates Peter had gotten for Christmas, with the big heels and shining blades; they weren't at all smooth like the girls' white figure skates. They were brown, and scuffed, and old, and the blades didn't look like much.

"So that's why he doesn't skate much," thought Peter. "He doesn't have decent skates!" One thing was certain, though: Mr. Adams did know how to skate. His laces were tied, all the way to the top, before the kids even had their shoes off, and he was on the ice in a flash.

"I'll be right back," he said, and skated right to the center of the pond. He made a few circles, checked the ice around the edges, and then motioned for the kids to come onto the ice. "All clear!" he called, and skated away.

Peter had thought he might impress Mr. Adams with his speed, and so he started to skate as quickly as he could; Jessica and Amy took hands and circled the ice a little more cautiously. It was bumpy, not at all like the ice at the rink where they had learned. They were looking down, trying to avoid the little cracks on the ice surface, and didn't even notice what Mr. Adams was doing. Until Peter skated over to them, took their arms and said, "Look! Look at Mr. Adams."

Mr. Adams was alone at the end of the pond, skating. He had thrown off his gloves and his jacket and was skating in nothing but a sweater and jeans, though it was still bitterly cold. He was spinning like a top!

THE SKATING PARTY

And gliding. He was twirling, now on one foot, now on the other. And he leapt in the air, from one side of the pond to the other in a single bound, as if he could fly. He was skating his heart out, and he seemed to have forgotten that the rest of them were there.

And they had forgotten that they were cold. The faster he skated and spun, the more remarkable he looked. His jeans turned white, his sweater turned white, he started to look like a dancing snowflake, a star. Maybe it was just the snow but he seemed to be getting whiter and whiter. And then he began to do partner skating—the kind where you lift a lady into the air. He seemed to be carrying an invisible partner—you could almost see her—then you *could* see her, another beautiful skater, dazzling as he was but not nearly so interesting, and another skater—were there three of them?

Amy and Peter and Jessica stood clutching each other's arms in disbelief. "It must be the snow," Amy muttered.

"Yeah," Peter answered.

Then the three of them looked at each other and said, "It's not the snow!"

"I don't believe what I'm seeing!" Amy whispered.

"Do you think he's going to, like, leap up into heaven or something?" Peter asked.

"I thought you didn't believe there was a heaven!" his sister whispered.

"C'mon, Jessica, give me a break! Don't tell me you don't see those other skaters?"

"Yes, I do see them," she said, graver now. "I thought maybe you didn't see them."

"We *all* see them," Amy said.

And then they were gone. Mr. Adams came whizzing across the ice to them, his hands outstretched. His garments were fading now; he looked the way he had before in his jeans and his sweater. But his eyes were glowing, and his cheeks were flushed; he touched them and his hands were warm, so warm.

Peter was the first to speak. "Wow, Mr. Adams, you could skate in the Olympics! We've got to get the other kids out here to see you. You could skate for the church! We could sell tickets! My dad's on the vestry—

THE SKATING PARTY

I'll get him to set it up. Wow, that was fabulous."

Mr. Adams' face changed. His eyes narrowed. He took Peter's hands in his. "Thanks, buddy, but I don't want to do that." He looked right into Peter's eyes. "I don't even want you to tell anybody."

There was a long silence. Peter couldn't believe his ears. The greatest skater he had ever seen—in the world probably—and he didn't want anyone to know. He didn't want people to know who he was. At last he nodded. "Okay, Mr. Adams. If you say so."

"So let's head back, huh kids?" Mr. Adams picked up his gloves and coat and put them back on, and took off the brown scuffed leather skates. The girls and Peter took their skates off and slung them over their shoulders. All the way home they were quiet. That was the way it had to be.

Jesus took with him Peter and James and John his brother, and led them up a high mountain apart. And he was transfigured before them, and his face shone like the sun, and his garments became white as light.

That's the story of the Transfiguration. Jesus took three of his disciples up on the mountain, and they saw something incredible. They saw Jesus changed; they saw that he was someone much more special and powerful than they had imagined; they saw two other teachers appear miraculously beside him. And when it was all over he told them not to tell anyone what they saw!

What did they see? What they saw was very special; it was real, but not like anything they had ever seen before. I think there must have been some change in the air, perhaps a shimmering; there might have been some special sound that they heard. I can think about it, but I don't know exactly what it was like. I do know that it was real, because they all saw it, and they told other people about it, finally, even though Jesus warned them not to. It was that real to them, and that special. If they weren't sure before that he was the Son of God, they had good reason to be sure now.

THE SKATING PARTY

What do you think they saw that day? What did it look like, up there on the mountain with Jesus? Was it like seeing Mr. Adams ice skate? Or was it better? Think about it!

THINGS TO THINK ABOUT

If you had been on the mountain with Jesus that day, what do you think you would have seen?

What would you have done?

Who would you want to tell?

Have you ever seen anything like what they saw on the mountain? What was it like?

PRAYING TOGETHER

Close your eyes and imagine yourself with the disciples, just before they see Jesus transfigured. What do they see? What do you see? What do the figures with him look like? Hold the picture in your mind for just a second.

"Lord Jesus Christ, you showed your glory to your disciples. Help us to glimpse it, even if only for a second; help us to pay attention to what we see. When we feel doubts about who you are, help us to remember what we saw, even if we only saw it once. Amen."

THE GREATEST

Then they came to Capernaum; and when he was in the house he asked them, "What were you arguing about on the way?" But they were silent, for on the way they had argued with one another who was the greatest. He sat down, called the twelve, and said to them, "Whoever wants to be first must be last of all and servant of all." Mark 9:33-35

It was the weirdest dream that Katie Johnson ever had. She dreamed she was waiting in line in front of an elevator with about thirty other high school kids. They were all waiting to ride the elevator. Beside the elevator was a big banner that read in white letters on red satin, "The Competition."

"Hey, what is this?" she asked the boy behind her.

"It's the line for the Competition. See, they give you this test—and, depending on how good you are, you get to go to a higher floor."

A bell rang at the elevator and some of the kids cheered.

"Wow, did you see that? Billy Proctor got to the thirty-fifth floor! He really must be good!"

Katie looked at the numbers above the elevator. Another kid got on. The doors closed. They all watched as the numbers on the elevator lit in turn—twenty, twenty-one, twenty-two. The kids cheered again.

"Twenty-two. Is that good?" Katie asked the boy behind her. But he was talking to somebody else. She tapped the girl in front of her, a girl she recognized from school.

"Hey, do you know what this is all about? What's on the test? What kind of competition is this?"

"It's to see who is the greatest. Didn't you know?"

"The greatest what?"

"You know, the BEST, the GREATEST. The ultimate!" Then she leaned over and whispered, "I think you're supposed to know a lot of vocabulary words. And have a lot of activities. You know, well-rounded."

Katie's heart sank. She hated tests. She thought, "Maybe she's wrong. Maybe it's just a physical."

THE GREATEST

Suddenly she was next. The man at the desk said: "Yes, step forward. Name, please."

"K-K-Katie Johnson," she said. And blushed. "Oh, nuts," she thought. "I hope we're not being graded for poise."

He handed her a card and said, "Give this to the operator." She froze. What about the test? Was that it?

She stumbled onto the elevator and said, "Up, please" in a thin little voice. The operator looked at her card and smiled, but said nothing. The doors closed, and the elevator started going down.

"Down? I'm going down?" She tugged at the operator's sleeve. "I'm sure there's some mistake!"

He looked at her card again, and smiled again. "No mistake, Miss." He stopped the car, opened the doors. "Here we are. Last door on the left."

Katie pulled her gym bag over her shoulder and squinted. "Great," she thought. "This is the sub, sub, sub-basement." It was dark. She moved along the hallway, one hand against the wall. She heard a voice down on the left. "Oh, good," she thought. "There's somebody else down here—maybe they can help me." She turned the corner into the last room on the left. She began to say, "Can you help me, please? There seems to be some mistake. I...." Katie stopped short. There, in a rocking chair, was an old woman.

"Oh." It was a tiny woman. She was so old, her skin was almost transparent. Her eyes were small. Her hair, white as white, lay flat along her head. Her hands were gnarled, and lay limp in her lap. Her feet dangled above the floor like a child's. Her sweater was dirty and old, and she wore tattered nylon stockings that bagged at her ankles. Katie had seen women like her when she visited her great-aunt at the nursing home.

She cringed. It didn't smell good.

All the time as Katie stared at the woman, the woman stared at her. Now she spoke. "Please," she said. "Take me home now, upstairs." She pointed up.

THE GREATEST

"Oh good," said Katie with relief, "I'm trying to get upstairs, too. Let's go together. I'll help you."

The old woman kept staring at her. "Comb hair," she said. Katie was puzzled. Was her hair messy? She touched her bangs. Hadn't she combed them just minutes ago? Then she realized that the old woman meant her own hair; she was to comb the woman's hair. "Sure, where's your comb?" Katie asked her. But the woman just went on staring, so Katie took the pink comb out of her own gym bag, and carefully parted and combed the old lady's hair. "Okay, let's go," Katie said.

But that was only the beginning. The lady pointed to her lips, so Katie offered her some lipstick, which she broke. Katie found a kleenex and helped to wipe the lipstick smudges away. Then she noticed that there was a button missing from her blouse; Katie fixed that with a safety pin. By the time they'd finished, Katie had even given her a pair of socks out of her gym bag which she, Katie, had to put on for her; the lady could reach her toes but couldn't get the socks on.

Kneeling to straighten the socks, Katie thought, "This is like dressing a baby."

"Now we go," the woman said.

"Fine. Where's your wheelchair?" The woman stared. No wheelchair. "A walker?" No walker. Katie looked in desperation for a cane. Not even a cane. "Can you walk?" she asked, staring again at those tiny feet, which were now wearing her crew socks as well as patent leather pumps so old the leather was cracked.

"Lift Mary," the woman said. "You strong. You carry."

Katie had had just about enough. She said, "Look, this is fun but it's all a mistake. I really have to get back to the competition. I'm missing some kind of TEST!"

She looked. Mary was smiling. "Lift Mary," she said.

"Oh, forget the test," said Katie, and leaned down to lift that old woman, who seemed so soft, a bundle of bones and satin skin. They went into the hall, and back to the elevator. Katie pushed the button hard. The doors opened. The light was all but blinding. Katie summoned all her courage

THE GREATEST

and said to the elevator operator, "Take us upstairs. And don't give me any business about a test. This woman needs to get home."

The old woman smiled and leaned against her chest. And then, in a voice clear as a bell, she said, "Well, Raymond, how's the competition going? Do you like my socks?" Katie gasped in surprise and the old woman looked at her. "You can put me down, dear." Katie put her down. "What's going on?" Katie demanded. "I thought you were helpless."

"Oh, not exactly," the woman answered. "You've done very well; you'd better take this," she said, and handed Katie something. Katie thought it was a dollar bill; anyway, she didn't look because she was staring at this woman, who was standing up tall now, and straightening her clothes. But there was something hard inside the dollar bill. When the elevator doors opened, Katie looked. It wasn't a dollar bill. It was just a piece of paper. But wrapped inside the paper was a pearl. And the paper read, "Thank you. The greatest."

JAMIE'S WAY

Katie woke up from her dream, clutching the tag of her pillow. In her hand, she found a pearl earring that her grandmother had given her. It had gotten caught in the tag. She sat up and rubbed her eyes. So that's what it was; her grandmother's pearl. But then she remembered the dream. She'd gotten out of the elevator, but what floor had she ended up on? Katie hadn't thought to look.

Some of Jesus' followers were wondering who among them would be the greatest. Jesus said, "The one who is greatest among you must be the servant of all." If you want to move up, go down. If you want to be the first, volunteer to be the last. Serve the littlest, tiniest, least important ones and you'll find out what really matters. That's what Jesus was planning to do.

What floor do you think Katie got off on?

THINGS TO THINK ABOUT

Have you ever been lined up for a competition of some sort? A try-out? What was it like?

How do you think Katie felt when the elevator took her to the basement?

THE GREATEST

What did you think of the old woman in the basement? How did you think she had gotten there? What was wrong with her?

Who did the old woman turn out to be? Where did she come from?

Do you think the dream had a message for Katie? What was it?

PRAYING TOGETHER

Close your eyes and think a minute: have you ever had to do a favor for someone when you didn't particularly want to? Imagine yourself doing just that—for an older person, or a younger brother or sister, or a friend. Now imagine that as you are doing that you are also wearing a badge that says, "The Greatest" on it.

"Lord God, you give us a life that is full of surprises. Help us to be ready to serve anyone you send our way, and not to worry about the competition. Amen."

Having It All

"Whoever is faithful in a very little is faithful also in much; and whoever is dishonest in a very little is dishonest also in much. If then you have not been faithful with the dishonest wealth, who will entrust to you true riches? And if you have not been faithful with what belongs to another, who will give you what is your own? No slave can serve two masters; for a slave will either hate the one or love the other, or be devoted to the one and despise the other. You cannot serve God and mammon." Luke 16:10-13

Janie Perkins had never seen a sweatshirt quite like the one Franny Williamson was wearing that day at school. It was sensational, that shirt. It was pink, with bits of lace, and silver sequins sewn about the front, and at the shoulders it had ribbons. It was very punk, that sweatshirt, but pretty at the same time. And when Franny Williamson wore it, with stretch pants, and her hair tied up in a ponytail, and big dangling earrings—well, she looked sensational. She just had it all.

At least Janie Perkins thought she did. She wanted to be like Franny; she wanted to be friends with Franny. Janie was sure that if ever Franny gave her a chance, and got to know her, she would like her. But it never happened. Franny Williamson never gave her the time of day. She always seemed busy with something or somebody else.

Janie figured, though, that if she couldn't hang out with Franny Williamson, maybe she could look as good. Hence the sweatshirt. She just had to have a sweatshirt like that one, pink, with lace and sequins and ribbons at the shoulders, punk but pretty, too.

So she went home and told her mother about it. Janie didn't just come right out and say she wanted the sweatshirt, because she knew if she did that, her mom might just say no. Instead she just talked about the sweatshirt, and even worked in something about how tidy Franny looked wearing it, even though it was big on her—she knew her mother would go for the tidy part. And when her mother mentioned later that she needed to go to Bloomingdales that day, Janie was ready to go in a flash. She kept her fingers crossed. If the shirt was anywhere at all, it would be at Bloomingdales.

As soon as they got off the escalator on the second floor of the store, Janie was sure she would find the shirt. It had to be there. Everything there was great! There was loud music, and these terrific little dancing dolls were hooked up and dancing on wires suspended from the ceiling, and there were neon lights—I'm not kidding—neon lights along the walls. "Sheeesh!" her mother exclaimed. "This place gets more like a discotheque every day. How can you think with all that racket going on?"

Janie just smiled. Yes, it was like a discotheque, more and more, and she loved it. She thought it was all a store should be. And then she saw it. There on a stand was a big TV with teenage girls modelling clothes from the store. And one of them was modelling the sweatshirt. There it was— deep pink, with sequins and lace and ribbons at the shoulder. Janie dragged her mother over closer to the screen. "See, Mom, I told you it was cool! It is such a great shirt. And it's only forty-five dollars!"

"Forty-five dollars!" her mother shrieked. "For a sweatshirt? You have got to be kidding."

HAVING IT ALL

Janie tugged at her mother's arm. "Oh, calm down, Mother, you've got that much, haven't you? I mean, look at that shirt. Isn't it great?"

Janie stared at the shirt so intently that she let go of her mother's arm. She was looking at one of the sequins, a shiny silver circle on the front of the shirt. She was staring at it because she was sure she saw a face in it, a beautiful, beautiful face. The longer she stared, the surer she was that she saw it. Not just a face, but a body too. It wasn't human. It was better than human—a beautiful, strong face on the body of an enormous fox. Its fur was sleek and settled about its face like a crown; its eyes were bright, its paws were delicately crossed.

The creature's head moved slowly round until its eyes caught Janie's and held her gaze. It was looking right at her, and now it filled the screen. It was a monster, actually. She knew that. She knew that she should probably be afraid. Yet somehow she wasn't afraid. She was entranced, enchanted. What a lovely, lovely creature. She couldn't take her eyes off him. She was about to turn to her mother and say, "Hey look!" when the creature spoke to her.

"Janie," it said. Its voice was beautiful. "Janie, I want to speak to you."

She gasped. It was talking to her! It knew her name!

"You want the sweatshirt. The pink one. I think you should have it, too. I'll get it for you."

Hey, she thought, this is great. Sounds like I've won a contest or something.

"Well, jeepers," she said out loud, "Thank you. That would be very nice. My mother said it was too much money. So thank you." She reached for her mother, but he spoke again.

"Is that all you want?"

"Excuse me?"

"Is that all you want? Is that all you want to have?"

"Well, no, of course not. I mean, it would be better if I had the stretch pants to go with it. In pink."

"Is that all you want?"

She gasped. This was too good to be true. "You mean I can have more?"

"Yes, you may have more."

"Well," she paused. "Well, Franny Williamson always wears her outfits with these cute little flats. They have bows on the tops and well, um, I just have loafers. So if it's not too much trouble, I'd like a pair of flats to go with the outfit. Actually, um, I don't want the flats with the bows. I like those lacy ones over there better. Would it be all right if I got both pairs? I'll take two. Please. Um, sir."

She paused a moment. Was this really happening? "Aren't I supposed to do something to get this?" she asked. "I mean, aren't you going to take my picture, or make me say, 'This is like no other store in the world,' or something like that?"

"Not really."

"What do you mean, not really? What's the catch?"

"Don't go away. Come a little closer. I want to see you. I want you to see some young friends of mine."

A little fearfully she edged closer to look. He arched his back, stretched, stood up, and turned so that she could see behind him.

"See! Here are my friends! I've given them everything they want—jewelry, clothes, cars, everything! They have everything they want. You can be like them, Janie."

Janie looked closer and saw that he was telling the truth. There were things there—toys, dolls, houses, cars, clothes, paintings. And there were people, too. They looked as if they had walked right off the floor of Bloomingdales into the television screen. They were wearing the most beautiful clothes; their hair was impeccably styled and combed; their jewelry matched their outfits; their shoes were new and stylish. "Wow," Janie thought, "I guess those are the models from the store."

But then she saw something that made her a little sick.

They had no faces. No eyes, no mouths, no noses—just blank, empty circles. There was no way to tell one from the other. Their clothes and heads moved as if they were real, but these people had no faces. It was as if they had disappeared inside their clothes. Just disappeared. Poof!

"Who are they?" she asked the creature.

"My young friends. The friends of Mammon."

Janie stepped back. She heard herself saying, "I don't think so," in a weak little voice.

"Oh, but you must!" whispered the creature.

Her voice was a little stronger now. "No. I don't think so."

"Oh, but you must! Think about the sweatshirt. Think about Franny Williamson. You need this, Janie. Really you do."

"I don't...." Janie faltered.

"Really, you need all of this. You know, you look terrible. You really do. Your clothes are shabby. It's no wonder you have no friends. You're a sight. You're not with it. I can help you, Janie. I can help you." His eyes were wider now, and he was glaring at her.

"I don't think so. I don't think so at all!" she replied. She heard herself saying it but she still couldn't move away from the television.

"Come on, Janie, you know me. I'm Mammon. I pay for your clothes, I set your hair, I make you popular. I give you jewelry. I make sure you can have pizza after school, a place to go in the summer time. I keep you happy. Without me you'd be nothing! You'd be out in the street! Nobody worth knowing would recognize you without me."

"What are you talking about? My mom and dad pay for all those things!"

"Not without me, they don't. I am money. My name is Mammon. You'll come around, Janie. You'll see how important I am."

"Mom," Janie said, reaching behind her. "Mom, I want to go home."

"What, dear?" Her mother had been behind her, looking at the prices on a pile of sweaters.

"I said I want to go home. Right now." Janie turned and looked away from the television screen. "Let's go."

"Janie, are you all right? What about the sweatshirt? I thought we were going to put together a new look for you today."

"Mom," Janie said, looking her mother straight in the eye. "It costs too much. Let's go get a coke."

"If you say so," her mother shrugged. "What were you looking at on that television all that time?"

"Oh, Mom, you don't want to know!" Janie said. And off they went.

HAVING IT ALL

"You cannot serve God and mammon." That's what Jesus told his disciples. By mammon, he meant money, security, the things you want. You can have what you need, and some of what you want; but you must never allow having things, or getting things, to be your main concern. Because if you do, you can get so caught up in the getting, and the having, and the keeping, and the getting more, that you lose your self. That's right, your very own self, your individuality, your very best self. Your soul.

"Trust in the Lord with all your heart," the proverb says, "and don't lean on your own understanding. In everything you do, acknowledge God, and He will direct your paths."

Everybody serves somebody. Some people serve things. They don't think of it that way, but if you look at what's most important to them, it's pretty obvious. The way around this is simply to choose to serve God instead. Since God has your best interests in mind, your best self, your soul, you actually gain the most by serving Him. If you trust God, and serve Him, you will have the things you need, and even some of what you want. There will generally be enough. It sounds superstitious, but it's true. The more you put your trust in God, the more you serve Him, the richer your life will be. More rich, more full of adventure than anything Mammon could work up. And that's a promise.

Incidentally, I thought you'd like to know that on the way home Janie Perkins and her mother found a great sweatshirt. It cost fifteen dollars, not forty-five, and it was black. Turns out Janie looks terrible in pink. With her red hair she looks terrific in black! Sensational! And you can see her face. You can really see it well.

THINGS TO THINK ABOUT

Do you have a favorite place to shop? What is it like?

Have you ever wanted something the way Janie wanted the pink sweatshirt? What was it? How much did it cost? Was there a friend who already had one like it?

What did you think of the monster, Mammon? What did he want Janie to do?

Why did the people in the TV not have any faces? What would it be like to have beautiful things and no face?

HAVING IT ALL

Was it hard for Janie to break away from Mammon? What do you think it took for her to get away?

Why did Jesus tell his disciples, "You cannot serve God and mammon?"

Why is it so important to get it straight about Mammon?

PRAYING TOGETHER

"Lord Jesus, you have given us a beautiful world. Most of the time we prefer things that we can see and have, but serving you is more important. Help us to know that. Help us not to be controlled by the things we want. Amen."

WHAT MARY SAW

After this I looked, and there was a great multitude that no one could count, from every nation, from all tribes and peoples and languages, standing before the throne and before the Lamb, clothed in white, with palm branches in their hands.

"These are they who have come out of the great ordeal; they have washed their robes and made them white in the blood of the Lamb.
They will hunger no more, and
thirst no more;
the sun will not strike them,
nor any scorching heat;
for the Lamb at the center of the
throne will be their
shepherd,
and he will guide them to
springs of the water of life,
and God will wipe away every
tear from their eyes."
Revelation 7:9, 14, 16-17

Mary was a sensitive child. At least that's what people always said about her. She wasn't sure what that meant; it made her look into the mirror to see if she was pale or sick or something. Maybe it was just people's way of being nice about the fact that she sulked a lot. She did—sulk a lot,

*W*HAT MARY SAW

that is. As far as she was concerned, she had a right to sulk.

Mary's parents were separated. Actually, they were divorced, but Mary would not use that word. She had promised herself never to give up the hope that they might get back together. So when people asked her, she would not say they were divorced, only that they were separated. "My dad doesn't live with us right now," she would say. In fact, her dad lived with somebody else—a woman Mary didn't like at all. The woman, whose name was Ilse, was all right, but Mary didn't like the fact that Ilse claimed to be married to Mary's father. "One life, one wife," Mary said to her dad. He didn't think it was funny.

Anyway, that's why Mary sulked a lot, why people thought she was "sensitive."

Mary had no brothers and sisters, and she never been especially popular at school. She went to birthday parties and was invited out sometimes, because her friends' parents made sure she was included, but it didn't help. Mary knew that the kids were just obeying their moms, who were friends with her mom. She knew that they wanted her to give up the sulking and accept the divorce. But Mary had better things to do. She *was* quiet, she *did* sulk a little; in her spare time she wrote short stories. And she was lonely.

Anyway, Mary was fourteen. It was autumn, and on an autumn night she saw something extraordinary.

It all started when she had a fight with her mother. They were making plans for Thanksgiving, and Mary's mother's idea was that she and Mary would go to a restaurant in a hotel for Thanksgiving dinner. They weren't going to have a turkey at home that year because her mom was working on a business deal and would have to be in Chicago right up until Wednesday night. Mary threw a fit. "If you want to go out for Thanksgiving dinner," she said, "why don't you just stay in Chicago? Why don't you order take-out food? I know, why don't you send a gift certificate to me and the housekeeper and we'll go out by ourselves? That would be just right—that would be just about the right size occasion for this family—me and the housekeeper."

"Mary," her mother said, "don't provoke me. If you'd rather go to your father's house...."
"Oh, Mom, you always want me to go over there. I don't want to. I want *my* family."
Her mother sighed. "Mary, we've been over this a thousand times. *That* family doesn't exist anymore. Your dad is starting a new family. This is your family. You and me."
Mary's eyes flashed. "Well, since we don't have any family now, maybe I'll go out alone." She whirled around, lifted her chin, and tossed an imaginary scarf over her shoulder as she strode from the room. She meant to look haughty, but her eyes were stinging with tears.
As she reached to push open the kitchen door, it dawned on her that someone else was in the kitchen—someone who had never seen her quite so ugly. There at the kitchen sink stood her mother's best friend, Joyce. Joyce was rinsing out a coffee cup and her mouth was open as if she wanted to say something, but couldn't get it out. Mary's mother was looking at Joyce, shrugging her shoulders. Mary hated that—the I-

don't-know-what-to-do-with-her-anymore look her mother had, and she went on through the door, embarrassed.

"Excuse *me*, Miss Mary!" Joyce called after her.

Mary stopped and smiled a little. Joyce liked to tease. Maybe it was going to be all right.

"Excuse me, Miss Mary, but I was going out to the store. You want to go for a walk?" Joyce was following her into the hallway. A walk, thought Mary. Maybe, maybe. She was pretty upset and maybe a walk would help. As she stood there thinking, Joyce caught up with her and gave her arm a little squeeze. "Come on, cutie, it will give your poor mother a break."

"Oh, all right," said Mary, trying to sound gruff. She didn't want to give up so easily. "I'll just get my jacket."

As she pulled it on she glanced at Joyce, who was busy adjusting the sleeves on her own jacket. Joyce was very particular about the way she looked. She was glancing in the mirror now, in fact, glancing over her shoulder to check the back of her jacket,

WHAT MARY SAW

tugging the hem down sharply so that it looked smart.

"Gee, Joyce, I thought you said we were just going to the store!"

"Well, you never know who you're going to meet." Joyce winked at her and they went out the door.

Outside it was just dusk. The air was chill. Between and above the buildings the sky was a deepening blue. Leaves snapped under their feet as they walked to a nearby grocer where the lights were bright. Joyce loaded milk and juice and English muffins into a basket, paid, and slid the change into a slim red wallet. Then she glanced at her watch.

"Oh, my God, Mary! I almost forgot. It's All Saints Day and I was supposed to be at church ten minutes ago. Look, I'll just drop you off at home—"

Mary's face fell. They'd only been out of the house ten minutes and she couldn't face her mother yet. "That's okay," she said quickly. "I'll come with you."

"Mary, are you sure? I know you go to church and everything, but All Saints Day is sort of extra credit. I mean, I just go because I'm, you know—"

"Because you're 'extremely religious,'" Mary said. "That's what Mom says. She says you're in church all the time."

"Oh, now, that's not fair. I'm not in church all the time, but I do go for special days like this. And I go when I'm feeling lonely, or when I miss my family."

By now they were just steps from the church. Mary was sorry; she would rather have kept talking and the evening air was so lovely. But it was time to go in. She was surprised to hear Joyce talk about feeling lonely; she had never thought of Joyce as lonely. True, she had never married and didn't really have any family in town, but she always seemed so perfect, so smart. Everything about her was slender and well put together. Mary, on the other hand, felt just plain puffy. How could Joyce be lonely?

"I don't get it, Joyce," she whispered as they stepped up to the pew. "If it's your family you miss, why don't you just go see them?"

WHAT MARY SAW

Joyce sat down. She took Mary's arm for a second and said, "Because they're all dead. I didn't have any brothers or sisters."

She knelt and put her head down, but then looked back over her shoulder. "When I'm here, I feel close to them."

Mary settled back in the pew and looked around. The church was dim except for candles at the front. After a moment the priest stood up and said that on All Saints Day we remembered all the people who believed in Jesus and were already with him—had died, that is—and we say special prayers for anyone who had died in the last year.

The service confused Mary a little. Just when she was getting used to the idea of all those dead people, they got up and baptized a baby. It was really cute, a tiny baby girl with wisps of black hair and pale hands, and that made Mary sad. She remembered there had been a baby after her, one her mother and father had wanted very much, who had died before it was born. She couldn't help wondering if that baby would have looked like this one, and whether her parents would have gotten divorced if the baby had lived. It made her think, too, of her grandfather, who had died the year before, and her Great Aunt Betsy, who used to make the best lace cookies and tell her silly jokes all the time.

Then it was time for communion. Joyce patted her on the knee and whispered that she was going up, but Mary didn't have to come unless she wanted to. But Mary did want to. The lights seemed brighter up around the altar, and she was growing curious about the little statues of the saints up there behind the altar. So she stood up and walked behind Joyce, folding her hands in front of her, and stood, and waited, and looked up at those little figures of the saints and into the stained glass windows, and drifted off, thinking. Might her grandfather have looked like one of them? Or the baby? She mounted the chancel steps, still thinking, and humming a little whatever hymn was being sung. Was it darker, or was that her imagination? The lights were warm and bright, but the air around her seemed dark.

That's when it happened. She saw them. Rather, she *felt* them. She felt as though there were people standing up next to her—

WHAT MARY SAW

behind her, on her right and on her left. It was almost as if they were carrying her, leading her all at the same time—her grandmother, her grandfather, the baby who had died; first she felt them, and then for an instant, only an instant, she saw them. They were like ghosts but they were real, all of them—the place was packed with them—old people, young people, women, men, babies.

They didn't seem unhappy, the way she'd heard ghosts do. They were all just leaning forward, looking up and they glistened...and she only saw it for an instant. As she made her communion, lifting the bread wafer to her mouth, she felt them still; when she tasted the wine, they were there. When she rose from her knees to go back to her seat she didn't feel their presence anymore, but she didn't mind. She felt such love from them! It was as if they were all there for her, even the baby whom she could hold and love.

Joyce was already kneeling when Mary got back to the pew. She knelt beside her, then put her hand on Joyce's shoulder. "I have to tell you something," Mary whispered. "I think I saw your family up there."

Joyce smiled, a big, goofy smile, and gave her a little hug. "I'm so glad!" Then she went back to her prayers.

About what Mary saw: she's not the only one. St. John, who wrote the Book of Revelation, saw it. Other people have seen it. You might see it one of these days. It's something that you would *see* with your heart, if you know what I mean. You just have to remember that sometimes the things you see with your heart are every bit as real as the things you see with your eyes.

But if you saw what Mary saw, what you would see is what we call "the Communion of Saints," all those people baptized in the faith who belong to the family of God. They gather in places like this because they love God, and we believe they gather especially whenever we celebrate the Eucharist. They are the "angels and archangels and all the company of heaven" the great prayer talks about. If you see them, and you may someday, you will probably be most aware of the ones you have already known. But there are many more. Ordinary saints, glorious

*W*HAT MARY SAW

saints, saints from long ago, saints who died just yesterday. More than we can know, they know that things are in God's hands and are going to be all right. That's what they showed to Mary, and what they can show to you.

It's going to be all right.

THINGS TO THINK ABOUT

What do you think Mary saw? How did she "see" it? Do you think other people saw the same thing?

What is a "saint," anyway? Can you think of someone in your family, someone who has died already, who was as important to you as a saint? What was special about that person? How do you remember them now that they're gone?

When people die, do we ever see them again? Can we talk to them? What do you think?

If Mary was a friend of yours, and told you about what she had seen, what would you think? What would you say?

PRAYING TOGETHER

Close your eyes and imagine yourself at a very long, very full dining table. Look around you and see the faces of the people that are there. Are these the saints? Is this like the group that Mary saw?

"God, we give you thanks for the communion of saints. Help us to remember that we don't ever need to feel alone. Amen."

A CASE OF DREAD

"There will be signs in the sun, the moon, and the stars, and on the earth distress among nations confused by the roaring of the sea and the waves. People will faint from fear and foreboding of what is coming upon the world, for the powers of the heavens will be shaken. Then they will see the Son of Man coming in a cloud' with power and great glory. Now when these things begin to take place, stand up and raise your heads, because your redemption is drawing near."

Then he told them a parable: "Look at the fig tree and all the trees; as soon as they sprout leaves you can see for yourselves and know that summer is already near. So also, when you see these things taking place, you know that the kingdom of God is near." Luke 21:25-31

Sarah Whitley opened one eye, looked at her alarm clock. Five minutes to seven, Monday morning. Oooh! she groaned. She pulled the covers back over her shoulder and pushed her head back up under the pillow, where it was cozy and warm. Somehow it seemed that under her pillow in her bed was the only safe place left on earth. Monday had finally come. In her bed it was safe and warm; outside it, trouble was waiting for her.

First, Mr. Martin, her algebra teacher, would probably be very angry with her today because for the third time she had not completed her homework assignment. She was afraid of Mr. Martin. When he was angry he was *very* sarcastic, and had a great way of humiliating girls in front of the rest of the class.

Two, she would have to face the librarian about her library book, now two weeks overdue. She was sure she had lost it.

Number three, she had to face a test in American literature given by the terrible Miss Peck, whom she feared and adored.

And of course she hadn't laid out her clothes the night before. Her gym clothes were still in her backpack where she had left them Friday afternoon after school (but we won't go into that).

"I can't tell Mom," Sarah thought. "She'll be mad. Re-e-e-e-ally mad." Now Sarah was developing a stomache ache, but there was no way out. She sat up in bed, she turned off the alarm before it rang. She got going.

She rolled out of bed and into her clothes. She ran from one end of the house to the other looking for the book, thinking about

A CASE OF DREAD

the algebra, muttering to herself. Sarah got lucky. The library book was buried under a pile of Sunday newspapers. The gym clothes were, well, smelly, but she shook them out, dusted some talcum powder inside them, and stuffed them into her backpack again. She gobbled down her breakfast and then on the bus—*on the bus*—she finished her algebra assignment. Not well, but she finished it, so Mr. Martin would have to wait for another day to make her feel bad.

As for Miss Peck's literature test, it wasn't as bad as she thought it would be. She had studied a little, not enough, but a little, and luckily most of the questions were about things she knew. It seemed she and Miss Peck were drawn to the same parts of *The Scarlet Letter*.

Sarah got through the day just fine. But at the end she was exhausted! She took herself in hand and said, "Listen, Sarah, that was a close call!" She imagined the lecture her mother would have given her had she known about the gym clothes. In the agonies of her imagination, she lived through what Mr. Martin would have said had he known about the homework and the bus.

She imagined the wrath of the librarian and, worst of all, the keen disappointment of the adored Miss Peck. Even without this lecture, she now knew what she could have done to make Monday morning okay instead of the awful experience she had gone through. She decided it was time to change her ways.

What Sarah was feeling that morning was dread. She hadn't been ready for what was coming. Some of it she couldn't have been ready for; it wasn't her fault that Mr. Martin was sarcastic when he was angry, and she couldn't really know what Miss Peck would have chosen for the literature test. But the library book and the gym clothes and the algebra homework—well, she could have done all of that on Sunday night instead of watching Star Wars. Now she realized that she was old enough to plan ahead. She suddenly understood what all the hectoring and lecturing on the part of her teachers and parents had been about. Things could go a lot more smoothly if you were prepared!

So much for Sarah Whitley.

A CASE OF DREAD

Jesus knew there would come a time when grownups and nations all over the world would feel the same kind of dread that Sarah felt on Monday morning, only much, much worse. That a day would come when grownups, grown men and women, would feel that their time was running out, and they would be so scared that they would be fainting with fear, wishing they knew what was about to happen. Wishing they were ready. Worrying about what was to come.

Some people think that when Jesus talked about the signs in the sun, moon, and stars, he was warning people about the end of the world. That's a scary topic! You can imagine it, can't you? It's what might happen if there were ever a nuclear war. Or if we can't find a way to repair the earth's ozone layer. If we can't grow enough food for the world's population. The world as we know it could just fall apart.

Of course we don't want to let that happen. We hope we have enough time to work things out. Some days that just seems impossible, and we get a worse case of dread than ever—what if we end the world ourselves? What if that's what Jesus meant—that the world would end, or blow up, or fall apart? Then we would meet him face to face, some of us not really prepared.

But of course Jesus was not talking about the end of the world and he wasn't talking about anything we can really control. He was talking about a time when he would return, when his kingdom would be real, when everyone would see him. He was talking about what will happen when God says "Time's up!" and we all get to meet him face to face. It's scary, but it's also exciting. Of course we want to see God, but we also want to be ready.

Times like Sarah Whitley's Monday morning are full of dread, for sure. But they are also great chances for us to change. Sometimes when you are scared, you're just about to get something right for the first time! After all, Monday morning is the beginning of a new week at school, or at work. Troubling times are also times of opportunity. Times when we can grow up, when we can change our ways, make new starts, get our act together as Sarah did.

A CASE OF DREAD

Jesus said, "There will be signs in the sun, moon, and stars, and upon the earth distress of nations, in perplexity at the roaring of the sea and the waves, men fainting with fear and foreboding of what is coming on the world. Now when these things begin to take place, look up, and raise your heads, because your redemption is at hand."

Well, what things are on your Monday morning list? Is there someone you want to be friends with, someone you've been meaning to call? Were there some good deeds on your list you haven't gotten around to yet? Are you worried about someone finding out that you haven't been doing your homework? Jesus said that if you're worried, it's time to fix it. Time for a change. The scary times may be the best times—dread can be the last thing you feel before you finally get it right.

When you see these things, look up! Your redemption is at hand. It's about to get better.

THINGS TO THINK ABOUT

Have you ever imagined the end of the world? What do you think it might be like?

Have you ever wondered what it would be like if Jesus came back and everyone could see him? Would everything change?

What things do you dread? What do you think it might mean to know that "your redemption is at hand"?

PRAYING TOGETHER

"Lord, help us to know when time is running out; help us to change our ways. If we need to forgive friends, help us to do it; if we need to say we're sorry, give us the chance to say it. If there are good things we want to do for other people, help us to get going. Teach us to know the signs of your coming, so that when you finally take the world into your care, we'll know that it will be well for us. Amen."

Jamie's Way

*Let the same mind be in you that was in Christ Jesus,
who, though he was in the form
of God,
did not regard equality with
God
as something to be exploited,
but emptied himself,
taking the form of a slave,
being born in human
likeness.
And being found in human
form,
he humbled himself
and became obedient to the
point of death—
even death on a cross.   Philippians 2:5-8*

No doubt about it, Jamie Matthews was rich. Her dad had a zillion dollars, probably, and they lived in an apartment so big she was sometimes embarrassed to have her friends over. "Wow!" they would say. "My whole house would fit in your living room." And things like that.

Being rich is nice. Jamie had a lot of dolls, and great clothes, and she got to go away skiing more than once a year, sometimes to Europe. The problem with it was that other kids sometimes misunderstood, and thought she was different from the rest of them. She wasn't sure whether she was different or not. She did know it wasn't quite normal to have the things she had. Not even at the private school she went to. Everybody knew she had the most stuff. Everybody.

Until the day she went into the hospital to have her tonsils out. Jamie's father and mother had taken her to the doctor the week before, and set the time for her operation; they had paid the hospital and promised her a special room, all to herself, on a special floor. They told her the room was on the corner of the hall, and had huge windows that looked out over the East River. The room even had wallpaper, and a rug, and didn't look like a hospital room but was more like a hotel. She only had to be there the night before the operation; she would have the operation early the next day, and go home very soon after that.

But the day Jamie went into the hospital, there had been a terrible accident downtown and all the rooms were full. Even her special room overlooking the river had been turned into a room for two adults, and the hospital said that under the circumstances the best they could do was to offer her a double room on the children's floor. In other words, no window overlooking anything, no rug on the floor, and she would have to have a roommate like most of the other kids.

Her father was furious. Jamie heard him out in the hall complaining to one of the nurses. "I give a lot of money to this hospital and I expect better treatment than this! This is an important operation! We were assured of a private room! How do I know that other child doesn't have AIDS or something?"

Jamie blushed until her face felt hot, and slid down under the covers of the hospital bed. Maybe she could pretend to be asleep, pretend not to be there. Why did her father always have to make such a scene? She could still hear him, could hear the nurse trying to calm him down, explaining that there was a shortage of rooms and nurses, a real crisis, and they were doing the best they could. The nurse sounded scared, as if she were holding her breath and waiting for this loud man to go away. "Oh, no," Jamie thought, "she's going to think I'm a spoiled brat now."

"Daddy!" she called out, even though her throat hurt. "Cut it out! I'm going to be fine! I like it here! My roommate's cute!"

She realized then that she hadn't even looked at her roommate. He was tiny—maybe two years old, tops—and fast asleep. And he was black. Oh, no, she thought, Daddy will make a stink about that, too, if he notices. Then people will really be upset.

She sneaked out of her bed and looked at the card taped to the foot of the little boy's crib. In purple letters, like the ones on her card, it said his name. Walter. Walter Green. He had white bandages around his hands and a little plastic tube, a clear one, coming from one of the bandages, was attached to a stand beside the bed. Walter was all scrunched down at one end with his behind in the air and his mouth open, sleeping soundly. She wondered what he had. It didn't say on the card. Maybe it was AIDS, or something terrible. But no, surely they wouldn't put them in the same room if he was that sick; after all, she was only having her tonsils out.

The nurse told Jamie and her mother that Walter's mother was sick, too, and his dad had to work, so there was no one to visit him. "That's terrible!" Jamie thought, and felt really sorry for him.

Little Walter was still asleep at eight o'clock when Jamie's mother said goodnight and went home. Jamie knew that she was supposed to go to sleep, too, but she couldn't. She was scared in the hospital. Everything smelled like the dentist's office, and the bed wasn't as nice as her bed at home. She was starting to wish Walter Green would wake up so she could play with him, but he didn't. The nurse came in a few minutes later and gave her a pill that helped; she turned on her side and went right to sleep.

Jamie slept soundly for awhile. But then, in the middle of the night, she was disturbed by a small voice from the other side of the room. It woke her up. "Ah-ah-ah-ruffff!" the voice called out. "Ah-ah-ah-ruffff!" She pulled back the green curtain that separated the two sides of the room and went to see what was the matter. Little Walter was sitting up, making these funny sounds, just playing really, but he was also pulling at the bandages around his hands, and tugging at the plastic tube. She didn't know much about medicine, but she had a hunch that if you had one of those plastic tubes you weren't supposed to pull on it.

She walked over to his bed and said, "Hey Walter, cut it out. You're not supposed to do that!" But he wouldn't stop. Jamie found a toy bear under the blanket at the end of the crib, and waved it in front of him. "Walter! Walter! Look at this!" but it didn't work. He looked at the bear for a second and then went back to pulling at the bandage. There was blood on it! Oh, no, she thought, and went quickly into the hall to see if she could find a nurse. There was a light on way down at the end of the hall, but she didn't think she dared leave Walter alone long enough to get there. Jamie pushed the nurses' call button, but got no answer.

She sighed and looked at Walter, who had begun to cry. He had pulled himself up to a standing position inside the crib and was banging the sore arm against its railing. There was only one thing to do. Jamie pulled the rocking chair up to the crib, climbed onto it, and leaned over to pull him out. Then she sat down in the chair, held him, and put her hand on the bandage to keep the tube in place. She was relieved to see that the blood on the bandage was old. Probably everything was still okay. If she could only get him to quiet down.

Jamie didn't know any lullabies. What was she supposed to do? So she sang other stuff. She started with "B-I-N-G-O," which didn't particularly interest him, but at least he wasn't crying quite so hard. Then she tried "Girls Just Wanna Have Fun," which bored him, but he did stop crying and started looking at her face. Then she tried "Jingle Bells." That made him giggle. It was such a treat to see him smile that Jamie sang it again. Then she thought, "Hey, I've got an operation tomorrow, I'd better get him back to bed so I can get some sleep!" She tried to stick him back in the crib. Nothing doing! Walter started wailing the minute she put him over the rail.

So Jamie sat back down. She would just have to get him to sleep first. Singing seemed the best thing to do—maybe she should sing something quieter. She tried

"Silent Night." That seemed to help. He stopped crying and nuzzled his head against her chest. That was better. Then she tried "Kumbaya": "Someone's singing, Lord, Kumbaya...." That seemed to do it. Walter was almost closing his eyes. "Someone's praying, Lord, Kumbaya." Then she remembered it was almost Easter, so Jamie sang, "Were You There When They Crucified My Lord?" "Oh-oh-oh-oh, sometimes it causes me to tremble, tremble, tremble." She sang and sang, thinking about Walter, and her operation, and how frightened she was, really, about going to sleep and having her tonsils out, but somehow it didn't seem as scary now. She held Walter, and hummed.

Hours later, when the nurses came in, they found Jamie and Walter still together in the rocking chair. It had been a terrible night: five more children had come into the Emergency Room, and the nurses had been so busy they hadn't gotten around to check on Jamie and Walter until the morning. What they found in Jamie Matthews' room, though, made it easier to take. She was holding Walter Green in the rocking chair, the two of them in each others' arms, fast asleep.

The nurses shook Jamie gently and woke her to take her back to bed. Drowsily she asked them to make sure Walter's bandage was all right, and they said yes, it was, and that she had done the right thing. They thanked her and said soothing things about how helpful she'd been. They also said that Walter's mother was better and would come in later that day to hold him herself.

When Jamie's mother came, Jamie heard the nurses talking in the hall again, saying how glad they were to have Jamie and how her mother could be proud to have such a loving girl. Jamie blushed and pulled herself under the covers again as she heard her mother say, "Yes, but that's Jamie's way."

Jamie's way. It was Jesus' way, too, though his was harder. Listen to what St. Paul said about it:

"Let the same mind be in you that was in Christ Jesus, who, though he was in the form of God, did not regard equality with God as a thing to be grasped, but emptied himself, taking the form of a slave....Therefore God also has highly exalted him and

JAMIE'S WAY

gave him the name that is above every name, so that at the name of Jesus every knee should bend."

That's the way Jesus was. And that was Jamie's way.

THINGS TO THINK ABOUT

Have you ever been in the hospital? What was it like?

Why was Jamie's father so anxious for her to have a special hospital room? Why did he feel that he could get special treatment for her?

Do you think Jamie was worried about the sort of disease that little Walter might have?

What did she do to help Walter? Why wasn't she afraid to help him?

What sorts of things has Jesus done to help us? Who is he more like, Jamie, or her father?

What does it mean, to "take the form of a servant?" Do you know anyone who does that?

JAMIE'S WAY

PRAYING TOGETHER

Close your eyes and picture yourself helping someone else, maybe someone who is sick, like Walter. Ask Jesus to help you.

"Lord Jesus Christ, you could have stayed in heaven and left us alone, but you didn't. When we needed help, you came to us. Come to us again and teach us to serve as you did. Amen."

*N*EVER LET HIM GO

At that hour Jesus said to the crowds, "Have you come out with swords and clubs to arrest me as though I were a bandit? Day after day I sat in the temple teaching, and you did not arrest me. But all this has taken place, so that the scriptures of the prophets may be fulfilled." Then all the disciples deserted him and fled.

Those who had arrested Jesus took him to Caiaphas the high priest, in whose house the scribes and the elders had gathered. But Peter was following him at a distance, as far as the courtyard of the high priest; and going inside, he sat with the guards in order to see how this would end.   Matthew 26:55-58

Allison Haymeyer was so frustrated she stamped her foot. "It was him!" she insisted. "I did see Tom Cruise yesterday, I promise!"

"Shhhh!" Mrs. Spackman warned from the doorway where the younger acolytes were lining up for church. "You girls are going to have to be quiet. The prelude has already started—hear it?" She turned back to eye the gang of girls on her left. "Allison, please come tie Janine's rope for her; it doesn't look right."

"Sorry, Mrs. Spackman," Allison muttered as she went to Janine and picked up the ends of the white rope belt. "She's right, Janine, this is a mess. Where did you learn these knots, Boy Scouts?" She yanked at the long white cord and started to retie the knots.

"Anyway," Allison continued, trying to keep her voice down, "You know that shirt shop at the mall? Right next to the yogurt place? He was standing right there, staring at the window. Gosh, he is so handsome!"

Sam Robinson stood next to her, and shifted his torch to one side. "C'mon, Allison, you really expect me to believe that? Tom Cruise is an actor, he's in the movies. He doesn't go to the malls in Pittsburgh—he lives in L.A!"

"Yeah, Allison," Nancy Rawlings chimed in. "Maybe you just saw a really handsome guy. I mean, what would Tom Cruise be doing at the mall?"

"Yeah," said Sam. "Besides, don't you think somebody besides you would have recognized him? I mean, where were the screaming girls?"

"Yeah, why didn't you get his autograph?" Nancy asked.

"Oh, I don't know. I was so surprised to see him, I didn't want to embarrass him or anything. Besides, it seemed so unreal. And, Sam, my dad says actors like Tom Cruise go out of L.A. a lot—to, you know, get ideas and stuff."

"What kind of idea are you going to get at the Hillandale Mall?"

"You just don't want to believe me!" Allison hissed.

She picked up the large processional cross and moved to the front of the line. Thank goodness the procession was starting—now they would have to stop bugging her. They would all have to concentrate on what they were doing, because, after all, this was Palm Sunday.

Remembering that it was Palm Sunday gave her a chill. It was Allison Haymeyer's first time ever as processional crucifer, and Palm Sunday was a major, major procession. All the way around the inside of the church, then up the main aisle. Usually only the oldest acolytes got to lead the processions, senior high school girls like Katie Reach and Mary Rockleberry, the rector's daughter. But Mary had the mumps, and

NEVER LET HIM GO

Katie was away for spring vacation, and after Mary and Katie, Allison was the Most Mature. She had to do it. She had been so excited she had talked her mother into a new pair of black patent leather pumps to wear with her vestments.

"Patent leather pumps!" her father had teased. "What next? White gloves? Tea at the Plaza? Or are you studying for the ministry?"

But here she was now, carrying the processional cross, the biggest, heaviest one, and singing "All glory, laud, and honor," but all she could think about was Tom Cruise. If it was really Tom Cruise, why was he alone? Why didn't anyone recognize him? Maybe Nancy was right—maybe this was just an incredibly good-looking guy. Maybe he just looked like Tom Cruise. She sighed, and lifted the cross to her waist.

Allison led the procession out and all the way around the church. She was lost in thought, so much that she lost track of the service. She put the cross in its rack at the front of the church and sat down, still in a kind of daze. When she started paying attention again the congregation was on its feet, reading the story of the Passion, the long section of the gospel that told about Jesus' death. Allison usually looked forward to this part; everyone in the church took part somehow, reading the different things that people said. She glanced around, trying to catch up. Janine's father was standing at the lectern reading the words that Jesus said, and Sam's mother was standing near the choir, reading what Pilate the judge said. The rest of the people were supposed to take the place of the crowds; that was the part she liked best. She found her place just as they all said, "Crucify him!" and she joined in the second time and said "CRUCIFY HIM!" Only she said it so loudly that she embarrassed herself and thought about Tom Cruise, in Pilate's court. Suddenly Allison wished the lines were different. She imagined herself on the sidelines instead, shouting, "Let him go! He's innocent, can't you see?"

Allison looked back at the leaflet. "GIVE US BARABBAS!" everyone was shouting. They were going to let a criminal go, and let an innocent man die! It was all a mistake.

Never let him go

They were so stupid! Why couldn't they see? Why couldn't they believe her?

She realized she was confusing Tom Cruise with Jesus. She was horrified. Tom Cruise was a movie star—Jesus got crucified. They were reading about it now. "I've got to concentrate!" she told herself. But she thought about him again. And what about Jesus? she wondered. Why didn't somebody stand up for him? If they knew he was king, if they loved him enough to make a parade the way they did, how could they turn around and kill him? How could they let him be killed?

It made her mad. "If I were there," she thought, "If I were there and Jesus caught my eye, if I saw him the way I saw Tom Cruise, even for a moment, just long enough to know who he was, I'd be loyal. I wouldn't let anybody hurt him. I'd stay with him. At least—I think I would."

It was time for communion, a busy time for acolytes. Allison did her job of helping at the altar and then went back to sit with Mrs. Spackman and the other acolytes. At least now she could relax, and think some more. There were so many people in church, it would be a long time before they all finished taking communion. Allison leaned back in her chair and stretched her legs. Then she thought of something.

"Mrs. Spackman," she whispered. "I have a question."

"Yes, hon, what is it?"

"Well, if those people knew who Jesus was, why did they kill him? I mean, why didn't the disciples stop it from happening? I thought they knew he was the Son of God."

"Well, not everyone did know who he was. At least, not that many were sure, deep down."

"But the disciples knew who he was!"

"Allison, the disciples were scared to death."

"You mean, they thought they'd be crucified, too?"

"Something like that."

"Oh."

Allison sat back in her chair and fiddled with her leaflet, thinking. Mrs. Spackman, too, was sitting back in her chair, and looking off into the distance. It was several minutes before Allison realized that Mrs. Spackman was humming.

"What are you singing, Mrs. Spackman?"

"Oh, just an old love song. 'Once you have found him, never let him go. Once you have found him....' It's from a musical called *South Pacific*. Don't know why I'm thinking about it today." She smiled, then touched Allison's arm. "Get your cross ready—it's time for the last hymn."

Allison picked up the processional cross once more and started down the long aisle of the church. The cross seemed somehow heavier than before, and the aisle seemed longer, too. And now they were singing such a sad song: "'Twas I, Lord Jesus, I it was denied thee, I crucified thee."

Allison noticed that some of the older people were wiping their eyes. Her own eyes began to sting; her chest felt warm; her hands were sweaty and she remembered what Mrs. Spackman had said. Some of the people weren't sure about Jesus, and some were afraid. She closed her eyes for a moment but kept walking, carrying the cross. And as she walked she prayed.

"Lord Jesus," she prayed, "sometimes I'm not sure about you, deep down, and sometimes I'm afraid. Grant that I may never let you go. Grant that I may never let you go."

THINGS TO THINK ABOUT

Do you think Allison really saw Tom Cruise at the mall? Why, or why not?

How could she be sure? What would be so special about it if she did?

If Jesus was the Son of God, why didn't everybody recognize him? Why were some of the disciples unsure about Jesus? Why would they be afraid?

If you were with Jesus just before he died, and you knew that he was innocent, what would you have done?

PRAYING TOGETHER

"Lord Jesus Christ, you come to us in many ways. Sometimes we believe that we have seen you, and know who you are; other times we aren't so sure. Sometimes we're afraid no one would believe us if we said it really was you. Help us to remember how uncertain your disciples were; help us not to let you go. Amen."

A SAVING GRACE

Jesus said to them, "Those who belong to this age marry and are given in marriage; but those who are considered worthy of a place in that age and in the resurrection of the dead neither marry nor are given in marriage. Indeed they cannot die anymore, because they are like angels and are children of God, being children of the resurrection....Now he is God not of the dead, but of the living; for to him all of them are alive." Luke 20:34-36, 38

It was the first Thanksgiving since the divorce, and Sherry gave it an F. A big fat F. Things at home had not gone well at all. Her mother found out that she had been drinking alcohol with her friends. She had also caught her smoking. But worst of all, she was on Sherry's back about her boyfriend, Chet. She had brought it up on Sunday, just as Sherry's older sister, Janet, was getting ready to go back to college.

"Sherry, I just can't believe you would be carrying on like this if it weren't for that boy," her mother said at breakfast. "He's a terrible influence on you—he smokes, he looks awful, he shows no respect when he comes into this house. How do I know he's not on drugs? Every time you see him you're out too late. Do you realize it was 3:00 A.M. when you came in last night?"

"Oh come on, Mom," Sherry had protested. "It was not—"

But her mother wouldn't let her finish. "Young lady, you and I will get along much better when you've stopped seeing that boy!" she announced, and left the room.

"Mother, you've got it all wrong!" Sherry called after her. "You don't understand about Chet at all!" No answer. "At least he loves me!" Still no answer.

Sherry sank back into her chair at the table and brooded, folding and refolding a paper napkin. How little her mother understood about Chet! He was so relaxed. He made her laugh. And he liked listening to her. They always stayed out late, usually talking. Well, all right they drank some too, but then, who didn't? Being sixteen was pretty hard for Sherry; it wasn't a great year, what with her parents getting divorced, and her sister leaving for college. But being close to Chet made things better, easier. Why couldn't her mother see that?

She wanted to say, "You flunk, Mom. F. Zero. Do not pass. This family deserves a failing grade."

But she didn't say that. She was tired of talking, just so tired. She never felt good anymore! So she went upstairs to help her sister pack, and offered to drive her to the train station. Anything to get out of the house. It was just too much. She thought they might talk in the car; she felt like crying, but nothing seemed to come. Not even words. So she just hugged Janet, hard, thinking, "I wish she knew how bad I feel! Nobody knows how bad I feel!"

"Bye-bye, Bobo," her sister said, using her oldest nickname. "Take it easy. I'll see you at Christmas." Sherry hugged her tight, until she felt something tugging at her shoulder bag, and so she pulled away. ("Wouldn't that just be perfect?" she thought, "I could get my pocket picked at the train station today. Just wonderful, like everything else.")

She put her hand on her bag, vowing to keep everything inside it, and watched the little windows of the train for her sister. When Janet appeared in one of them and waved, she waved back and turned to go back to the car. She still felt awful. She was wondering if there was anything left in the rum bottle she'd hidden under the front seat; maybe she could polish it off before she got back to the house. Anything would feel better than this.

Sherry got to the car and reached under the seat for the bottle. Yep, there were a few drinks left. She slunk down behind the driver's seat so she could have a drink without being noticed, and slipped her hand into the outside pocket of her bag for a cigarette. There was something on top of the cigarettes, and she pulled it out to look at it: a long white envelope with her sister's loopy handwriting on the front—"To Sherry. Open now."

She lit a cigarette, took a swig from the bottle and opened the envelope. "Dear Bobo," it read:

"You seemed so unhappy at home this weekend, that I thought I ought to say something. (You probably thought I didn't even notice! I just didn't know what to say. Sorry!)

"There's something I have to tell you, and it's about my accident last year. (I know, I've had a lot of accidents, but I mean the Big One, when I totalled the car.) Well, it wasn't really an accident. I veered off the road on purpose. I wanted to die. It seems silly, now, but Dad and I had a MAJOR fight, about him dating that idiot Joyce. (Remember her? Awful!) And then I tried to call him at his office the next day and he didn't call me back. I was so upset, I thought he'd just forgotten about me, and I couldn't stand it.

"Anyway, like I said, I wanted to die. I thought that would fix everything. Daddy would know what a jerk he'd been, and I would be out of my misery, and everything would be all right. And if it didn't work, well, I figured at least Daddy would know how upset I was.

"The reason I'm telling you this now is so you won't try it! Because after I did it, I didn't want to die anymore. It wasn't because I was scared to die. I was too mad at everyone to be scared, and rolling the car—well, it happened so fast I don't remember much.

"What I do remember is this—while I was out there, almost dead, I saw God. Don't laugh! I'm serious. I saw that funny light they talk about in the movies and I saw the tunnel leading to it. I saw just enough to know that it was peaceful, over there, on the other side, and that it would be okay to get there and stay. It would make things all right for me, just as I had imagined.

"But then the funniest thing happened. Once I saw it, I didn't want to go anymore. It was as if I could look back at my life and see that it was still awful: I was still mad at everybody and sick of school and worried about exams and everything. But I wanted to go back anyway. That's when I saw God—or rather I heard Him. You know what He said? He said, 'We don't have to do this right now, you know. Why don't you wait and come back another time?'

"And I said yes, just like that.

"Isn't it funny? My problems were all still there, and I knew that, but somehow I felt that God was giving me a break. Like I could die, or live—either way would be all right, really all right—but He would let me choose.

"Then He said, 'You'll always be alive to me, Janet.'

Isn't it funny? I didn't really believe in God before this happened. I mean, I went to church and got confirmed and all, but it all seemed so unimportant. I couldn't see what all the fuss was about. But now that's changed. I guess you could say I'm a true believer. (Don't get me wrong, I'm not going to become a nun or anything!) But I am going to be Janet-who-believes-in-God. I already am. It's made all the difference.

"The reason I'm telling you all this now (please, please, don't tell anyone else) is that you seemed so bent out of shape over this vacation, I thought you might try the same thing. Believe me, it isn't worth it. Concussions really do hurt, and it isn't fun being in a hospital, and besides, I like having you around much too much. I love you—a lot—and I want you to be happy. Bad times pass. Believe it. I love you, and I'll see you soon. Janet."

Sherry was crying when she put the letter down, wiping tears with the back of her hand. She had tossed her cigarette out the window; there wasn't much left in the liquor bottle, but she thought with a little care she could make it home all right. No, she thought better of that. She pulled her bag out, got a quarter, and called her mom at the phone nearest the parking lot. "Mom," she said, "I'm leaving the car here and going to take a cab home. I had a drink and I don't think I should drive." She didn't give her mother time to say anything; she was sure her mother would have plenty to say when she got home. She hung up, checked to be sure the car was locked, and found a cab to take her home. If Janet could stay alive, she could do it, too. She could do it, too.

In Jesus' day some Sadducees—people who didn't believe you could live after you died—some Sadducees gave Jesus a trick question. They were trying to show that a life after death didn't make sense, so they asked him this: if you die and go to heaven, and you've been married more than once, whose wife are you then?

Jesus told the Sadducees that they had it all wrong. He said that people who live again after they die don't just pick up where they left off and go on in heaven as if nothing really happened. He said they're changed, like angels.

Sometimes people who try to kill themselves don't understand about the resurrection of the dead. They think that if there is a life after death, it must be like this one, more or less. So by killing yourself, you could get your life back. As if you could pay back all those people who hurt you, and still be around to see them change their ways. But it doesn't work that way. Jesus made it clear: when we are raised we are changed. It's a different sort of life. Wonderful, yes, but very different from the life we're living now.

And the life we're living now is good enough for the time being. We can be with God right away; we don't have to wait for death to do that. God is God of the living, and that means us. Even if life is miserable, we know that bad times pass. And God is with us, even in the bad times. You don't have to kill yourself to find Him. Or to find out what life is really about. You don't have to look further than your own troubles to find God; you can ask Him for help right away.

So if you're about to give a big fat F to your life—maybe you have problems at school, or at home, or at work—think again. You could try to meet God the hard way, by giving up, or you could ask for His help right now. It's much easier! And you can wait to find out what the other life is like, because there's plenty of time for that. No matter how bad things seem now, God can help you work them out. Maybe you're like Sherry, and you have a sister or brother who'd like to help you. Or maybe an older friend—a teacher, an aunt or an uncle. Maybe even your mom or dad. Talk to them, and keep talking! If they don't understand, talk to somebody else. And whatever you do, keep talking to God.

Reach out, before you check out! Don't look into the next life, until you're satisfied with your life with God in this one.

THINGS TO THINK ABOUT

Have you ever known someone who tried to commit suicide? What happened?

What kinds of things make kids want to kill themselves? Do you think they really mean to kill themselves?

What would you do if you knew that a friend or family member was considering suicide? What would you say to them?

PRAYING TOGETHER

"Lord Christ, sometimes we wonder if dying would be better than living. Help us to cope when we feel this way. Help us to know that you are the God of the living and care about us right now. Teach us to live. Amen."

THE PEACE OF CHRIST

Jesus answered him, "Those who love me will keep my word, and my Father will love them, and we will come to them and make our home with them....I have said these things to you while I am still with you. But the Advocate, the Holy Spirit, whom the Father will send in my name, will teach you everything, and remind you of all that I have said to you. Peace I leave with you; my peace I give to you. I do not give to you as the world gives. Do not let your hearts be troubled, and do not let them be afraid." John 14:23, 25-27

On Grandmother Ritchie's porch, there was always a place to sit. "That porch is half the house," she used to say, and she meant it two ways: the porch was half as big as the house, and almost as important. Summer evenings after dinner Grandma always went out there to sit, and talk, and listen to the closing of the day.

That porch was one of Jamie's favorite places. Every summer when her mother took her down to stay with her grandparents in Florida, she looked forward to those evenings on the porch. Soon as the dishes were resting in the dishrack—she wouldn't bother drying them with a towel—

The Peace of Christ

Grandma would go out the front door, smooth the back of her cotton skirt to keep it from wrinkling, and sit down in the green metal armchair nearest the railing. And there she would stay, sometimes until it was dark, talking, fanning herself with a paper fan, watching the world go by and the day go dim.

When she was little Jamie would run out into the grass to catch fireflies in a jar. Once, when she and her cousin Keith were eleven, they tore up the lawn making a crazy golf course out of the croquet set. Aunt Elsie had screeched about that and all the grass they'd dug up, but Grandma had only raised her eyebrows, smiled a second, then gone back to her knitting as if nothing had happened. The last summer or so, though, Keith was always out riding bikes with the other boys in the neighborhood, and Jamie preferred to stretch out on the long glider couch and listen, with Grandma.

She loved to listen out there: screen doors slamming up and down the block, Mrs. Bledsoe hollering for her sons to get inside for dinner, old Mr. Grant whistling for his dog to come in. Grandma would rock ever so slightly in her chair and take up her knitting, and when the light failed her, put it down and start to hum. That was Jamie's favorite part. Grandma seemed to forget that anybody might be listening, and she would hum, then sing, the old hymns. Hymns they didn't sing in Jamie's church in New York, hymns she never heard except from Grandma, and sometimes at the Baptist church she took them to when they visited. Hymns like "The Old Rugged Cross," and "I Come to the Garden Alone," and "I Need Thee Every Hour." One Jamie liked especially, though it was sad:

> When Jesus comes,
> The tempter's power is broken;
> When Jesus comes,
> The tears are wiped away.
> He breaks the gloom
> And fills the world with glory,
> For all is well,
> When Jesus comes to stay.

It was puzzling to Jamie, that hymn. It talked about all the tears being wiped away, but every time she heard her grandmother sing it, it made her want to cry. Actually it

THE PEACE OF CHRIST

made her want to crawl up in her grandmother's lap again, the way she used to. Now she was much too big to do that—five feet seven inches, in fact—and too grown up. No, she couldn't sit on Grandma Ritchie's lap on the porch anymore, or bury her head on that shoulder, or catch the little bit of perfume that Grandma liked to dab behind her ears.

One night she and Grandma stayed out there listening and talking long after the others had gone. Jamie's parents had gone to town for dinner, and Grandpa had gone to bed early, and Keith and his parents were off at the beach overnight. They talked about everything under the sun. About learning to ride a bike, about girls and skirt lengths and modern hair styles. Grandma told her about meeting Grandpa at a church supper when he was seventeen, and she was only twelve, and how she hoped he'd wait until she was grown up and marry her, and he did. She even told Jamie about the time on a vacation when Grandpa got so seasick, out on a sightseeing boat, that he promised God if he ever got home and felt better he'd give the Baptist Church a hundred dollars, and he did.

"Grandma," Jamie said, "I really like it here. I wish I could just stay with you. Maybe I could even move down here and go to Jacksonville High with Keith! I could help you with the house, and everything!"

"Well! That's quite an offer, young lady," her grandmother said. "And just what is it about this place that you like so much that you'd leave New York City to have it?"

"Well I don't know, it's just so, so peaceful!" Jamie replied.

"So it's peace you're after, eh? Peace and quiet, or just peace?"

"What's the difference?"

"Oh, you'll know one day. You'll know. Come here a second." Jamie felt her face feel hot. Oh no, she thought, what's she going to do? But she got up obediently and went to her grandmother's chair. "Come down further so I can reach you without straining," her grandmother said. And she did. Grandmother Ritchie put both her big hands on Jamie's forehead, and held them there a minute before she said, "Lord Jesus, give your peace to Jamie just as soon as

THE PEACE OF CHRIST

she's ready. For your tender mercy's sake, Amen."

Jamie felt her grandmother's palms cool against her skin. They moved from her forehead to her cheeks in a light caress before her grandmother sat back and folded those wrinkled, spotted hands in her lap.

Jamie shivered and straightened up. She looked quizzically into her grandmother's face for just a second, then got embarrassed. What was that all about, she wondered. All that business about Jesus. "Goodnight, Grandma!" she said awkwardly, and slipped back into the house to her room, and went to bed.

That night Jamie had a dream. She dreamed she was back in New York, walking in Central Park with some friends. They went over to the Sheep Meadow, the great green lawn where the picnickers go, and saw all the usual sorts of people sunbathing, and playing radios, and reading books. But something was different. This time there were also sheep and cows grazing in the meadow, right out there with the people, and no one seemed to think it was in the least bit unusual. And right in the center of the meadow was Grandma's porch, standing all by itself.

Grandma stood on the porch waving to her, so Jamie went right to the porch and stretched out on the glider the way she always did. But when she did, the noise in the meadow got louder and louder, until she couldn't hear herself think. Then there was a bump, and the glider jolted beneath her. There was a fight breaking out right beside the porch, between some kids—some of them white, some of them black—and they were bumping into the porch, nearly falling onto her. Jamie was terrified. She pushed them away and struggled up and looked at her grandmother in alarm. Grandma just walked over, put her hands on Jamie's head, and said "Blessed child!" And kissed her.

Jamie said goodbye to her grandmother and left the porch. She didn't feel afraid anymore. The noise was still very loud but it didn't trouble her so. When she woke up, she was saying, "It's going to be all right; I've got the porch. I mean I've got the peace."

*T*HE PEACE OF CHRIST

Next morning Jamie found that her grandmother had been taken to the hospital in the night. She had been feeling very strange, and old as she was, they couldn't take any chances. She had stopped in Jamie's room just long enough to kiss her, and say goodbye. Everyone was worried, because she'd said goodbye to them all, even to the house. As she walked down the sidewalk to the car she'd turned back and said "Goodbye, sweet house." Grandpa thought something must be terribly wrong for her to say that.

But Jamie—Jamie knew it was going to be all right. Even if her grandma died, it would be all right. And she thought she'd learned something from the dream. Peace, the peace of Jesus that Grandma was talking about, wasn't the same as peace and quiet, it wasn't just resting on the porch at the end of the day and feeling calm. It was knowing, even when it was noisy and scary and you didn't feel particularly good, that everything is going to be all right, somehow. That all will be well.

Grandma knew that. Grandma had the peace of Christ. And she'd wanted it for

Jamie. Just knowing that made Jamie feel better.

Jesus said, "Peace be with you; my peace I give unto you; not as the world gives, give I unto you. Let not your heart be troubled, neither let it be afraid."

THINGS TO THINK ABOUT

Do you have a favorite, peaceful place? Where is it, and what makes it special? When do you get to go there?

What sort of person was Jamie's grandmother? When she put her hands on Jamie's head, what did you think she was going to do? Have you ever known anyone like that?

Do you think Grandma Ritchie thought she was going to die when she left the house? How about before, when she gave the peace to Jamie? If she thought she might be dying, why was she so calm?

Can we have the peace of Christ? What do you think it is? How do we find it?

PRAYING TOGETHER

Close your eyes and think of your favorite, peaceful place. If you like, silently

THE PEACE OF CHRIST

invite Jesus to visit that place next time you're there.

"Lord Christ, thank you for giving your special peace to your disciples. I would like to know that peace, too, and give it to others that I know. Give me your peace as soon as I am ready. Help me, when I have it, not to be afraid. Amen."

Cowley Publications is a ministry of the Society of St. John the Evangelist, a religious community for men in the Episcopal Church. Emerging from the Society's tradition of prayer, theological reflection, and diversity of mission, the press is centered in the rich heritage of the Anglican Communion.

Cowley Publications seeks to provide books, audio cassettes, and other resources for the ongoing theological exploration and spiritual development of the Episcopal Church and others in the body of Christ. To this end, it is dedicated to developing a new generation of theological writers, encouraging them to produce timely, creative, and stimulating publications of excellence, and making these publications available widely, reaching both clergy and lay persons.